Somewhere More Holy

Stories from

A BEWILDERED FATHER

STUMBLING HUSBAND

RELUCTANT HANDYMAN

AND PRODIGAL SON

TONY WOODLIEF

ZONDERVAN®

ZONDERVAN.com/
AUTHORTRACKER
follow your favorite authors

ZONDERVAN

Somewhere More Holy
Copyright © 2010 by Tony Woodlief

This title is also available as a Zondervan ebook.
Visit www.zondervan.com/ebooks.

This title is also available in a Zondervan audio edition.
Visit www.zondervan.fm.

Requests for information should be addressed to:
Zondervan, *Grand Rapids, Michigan* 49530

Library of Congress Cataloging-in-Publication Data

Woodlief, Tony, 1967 –
    Somewhere more holy / Tony Woodlief.
       p. cm.
    Includes bibliographical references.
    ISBN 978-0-310-31993-1 (softcover)
     1. Christian life. 2. Woodlief, Tony, 1967 – I. Title.
    BV4501.3.W658 – 2010
    277.3′083092 – dc22
                                         2009051038

Unless otherwise indicated, all Scripture is the author's paraphrase.

Any Internet addresses (websites, blogs, etc.) and telephone numbers printed in this book are offered as a resource. They are not intended in any way to be or imply an endorsement by Zondervan, nor does Zondervan vouch for the content of these sites and numbers for the life of this book.

All rights reserved. No part of this publication may be reproduced, stored in a retrieval system, or transmitted in any form or by any means — electronic, mechanical, photocopy, recording, or any other — except for brief quotations in printed reviews, without the prior permission of the publisher.

"Perhaps the World Ends Here" from THE WOMAN WHO FELL FROM THE SKY by Joy Harjo. Copyright © 1994 by Joy Harjo. Used by permission of W. W. Norton & Company, Inc.

For additional credits, see page 205.

Cover design: *Michelle Lenger*
Cover photography: *Michael Bankston*
Interior design: *Michelle Espinoza*

Printed in the United States of America

10 11 12 13 14 15 /DCI/ 21 20 19 18 17 16 15 14 13 12 11 10 9 8 7 6 5 4 3 2 1

Brother Buechner, Father Buechner, your voice cries out in a world that wants no prophets. You have more children than you know, and we are grateful.

Because all peddlers of God's word have that in common, I
think: they tell what costs them least to tell and what will gain
them most; and to tell the story of who we really are and of the
battle between light and dark, between belief and unbelief,
between sin and grace that is waged within us all costs plenty
and may not gain us anything, we're afraid, but an uneasy
silence and a fishy stare.

Frederick Buechner, "The Two Stories"

The old house will guard you,
As I have done.
Its walls and rooms will hold you,
And I shall whisper my thoughts and fancies
As always,
From the pages of my books.
You will sit here, some quiet Summer night,
Listening to the puffing trains,
But you will not be lonely,
For these things are a part of me.
And my love will go on speaking to you
Through the chairs, and the tables, and the pictures,
As it does now through my voice,
And the quick, necessary touch of my hand.

Amy Lowell, excerpted from "Penumbra"

our father reads to us. We laugh out loud.
No pictures, just a curly crowd
of letters we will learn. The squiggles mean
trout streams under our living room, a bean
stalk, some goats, a cloak lamplight unfurls.
We're listening, Dad. We're sounding out whole worlds.

Jeanine Hathaway, "IN THE BEGINNING"

Introduction

the doorstep

I am standing outside my own front door, girding myself for battle. I am home from another fruitless day in a job that I hold down because it pays the bills. All I want, really, is a beer and a foot rub. Instead I am about to be the target of crotch-level flying tackles from my children. In these moments it helps to pause, and collect one's thoughts, and try to remember what one learned in karate class years ago about deflecting groin strikes. I know they don't mean any harm by it. This is how they show they love me. There are many definitions of *home*, and perhaps this is one of them: *the place where sometimes we are wounded.*

I often come home to the sound of activity, the bustle of four children wrestling and giggling and arguing, and at the center of this hurricane, their mother, Celeste. She is the one who maintains peace in my absence. She is slowly, methodically, civilizing them, and without going stark-raving mad as I would have done were I left alone with these little barbarians every day. For a moment, as the door's creak echoes in the foyer, there is silence. They are pausing, listening. This is followed by shouting, and little feet stomping across floors and up or down stairs at breakneck speed, which always feels like a cross between a sentimental reunion and that scene in *The*

Lord of the Rings where the shrieking Orcs come charging up from the depths of their caves.

At the sight of me the littlest ones dance and clap their hands before clamoring to be held. My six- and eight-year-olds don't tarry; they barrel forward to deal out that combination of assault and hug that is an instinct of small children, and especially of little boys. Their mother usually smiles and sometimes hugs me or kisses my face. Here is another definition of home: *the place where they embrace me regardless of my failures.*

My wife and I grew up yearning for a home. Neither of us lived in places fit for children. I hesitate to say so because a careful peace has been worked out in our families—a peace based on the fundamental principle that families don't talk about what's wrong, and especially about who did what to whom. I am going to break that peace now. And I'm going to do it in a cowardly way, no less, by telling you about it rather than accusing the perpetrators directly. Perpetrators. That is often what we parents become to our children, in small and sometimes frightfully large ways. We adults write many of the stories that unfold in our homes, but our rooms also harbor the ghosts we inadvertently packed up and carried with us from our childhoods. One of the things Celeste and I have learned about building a home is that it will never feel safe until you scare your ghosts out into the open.

Our home, for example, is strikingly neat, considering the terror-inducing reality that we live with four boys under the age of ten. In the battle between chaos and order that rages daily under our roof, you might be surprised to learn that order wins quite decisively. Everything has a place, and you get in trouble when you forget that. No dinner until your room is straightened. Pick up the Legos strewn about the table where you built your supergalactic invisible spaceship. Unstack all the chairs you used as a barricade against your baby brother. If your shoes are left in a little pile in the hallway instead of placed in the closet, you're going to get a stern talking to.

Sometimes my children look to me for relief from their mother's strictures, but I tell them that they don't even know the half of it; I share a room with the woman. It wasn't until I got married, for example, that I discovered there is a wrong way to put the toilet paper on the spindle. And I can't tell you how many times all the books and magazines and pens populating my nightstand have been unceremoniously swept into the top drawer. I think it's fair to say—and in her calmer moments she acknowledges this—that Celeste is overly strict about how we organize our home.

The ghosts intrude when you are trying, as Celeste and I are, to build a home out of nothing. Her incessant quest for order is a consequence of sexual abuse at the hands of her stepfather. Her father had died when she was four, and her stepfather began molesting her when she was ten. Rather than fetching a shotgun and running her molester out of town, Celeste's blood family failed to protect her. Her own mother made excuses for the man, who promised to seek counseling. He kept his hands to himself for a while, and everyone pretended that things would henceforth be normal. The message Celeste received from her relatives, especially her mother, was blunt and painful: *you aren't worth it.*

Celeste's stepfather didn't stop. I met her when I was sixteen; she was fifteen. Her stepfather had left her alone for a time, but now he was making advances again, in the way predators do. He had taken to whispering lewd comments, and touching her inappropriately. He was testing the defenses, to see if she would accuse him again. When I was seventeen, she told me about him.

Later that summer, in the darkest part of night, I drove my battered VW Bug to the end of Celeste's street. She stood clutching a suitcase and crying. I took her to her grandfather's house, where she said she'd be safe. I felt like a hero, like I had saved her. I wanted to protect her for the rest of our lives.

Celeste's relatives moved her from home to home after that, nobody wanting the responsibility of a broken-hearted teenage girl for very long. She lived in seven different places during her high school years. It was always borrowed space — a bedroom, a basement — and sometimes it was painfully clear that she wasn't very welcome. Once she came back to her aunt's house, where she had been staying, to find her bags packed. Her uncle was worried that she might accuse him of molestation too, as if she leveled accusations like that for the fun of it. Other relatives were more caring, but always there was the steady reminder that she was the cause of dislocation.

I noticed that wherever she lived, whatever corner she found herself in, Celeste kept it neat. She stacked plastic milk crates to serve as a dresser and bookshelves. She kept her favorite pillows neatly arranged on whatever bed she was provided. Her shoes were arrayed straight and orderly in her closet. She tried to organize me too, hopeless as that endeavor has proven to be.

There were other curiosities about Celeste that only later did I realize were connected to this obsession with order: she ate the food off her plate one item at a time; she needed exactly the same amount of dipping sauces when she ordered chicken nuggets; she got terribly upset if she lost a hair bow; she kept her music tapes in alphabetical order by musician's last name. She always needed to know the schedule; she could never just hang out and see what happened.

I used to make fun of her, not knowing what I understand now, which is that these were the ways she kept a piece of her world in order while the rest of it came undone. While girls her age worried over prom dresses and senior photos, Celeste tried to figure out where she would sleep and how she could convince her mother to sign a form authorizing her to get her dead father's last name back.

Neatness means order, and order means control, and control means that people can't hurt you. It means that you belong in the space you occupy. These things are easy enough to see now, but it took me years to figure them out. An orderly home, to Celeste, isn't just some old-fashioned, Martha Stewart fetish. It is survival. It's how she reminds herself that she doesn't live in that place where she grew up. Seeing her struggle, I have learned another definition of home: *that place where we feel safe.*

Celeste and I know that our children will probably be uptight as a result of this constant striving for order. I suspect that one day, when they come to understand it, our boys will agree with me that the fuss was worth it. In knocking ourselves out to keep the bins and baskets and canisters that populate our home properly stocked and ordered, we afford this woman whom we all adore a measure of peace. This is one of the ghosts that whispers in our home, the ghost of her childhood.

While Celeste's real father was killed in a car accident, I ended up with an adoptive father because my real father left. He and my mother divorced when I was young, and I stopped seeing him altogether when I was seven. Years later, I learned that my mother had told him I was being mocked by the other schoolchildren because my last name was different than her new last name. She wanted to have me adopted by her new husband. My father acquiesced to her demands, and soon after I stopped seeing him altogether.

I don't remember any mockery in school; I think my mother just wanted a tidy new family, and my father had become an obstacle to that fantasy. I'm sure everyone's perception, especially that of a seven-year-old boy, is cloudy in such situations; but here is the undeniable reality: like many other children, I received the message at a young age that my father didn't want me.

My replacement father, meanwhile, was a rough, angry man. He was, in many ways, everything I thought, even into adulthood, a man is supposed to be. He was an ex-Green Beret, a decorated combat veteran of the Vietnam War. He was a pipefitter by trade, and he raced cars as a hobby. He had a deep, booming voice and hands that felt like iron, at least when they were striking you. The most important lesson I learned from him came very early, and it stuck: *stay out of the way.* I suppose he was fighting his own demons, between a war and an abusive father of his own. The world doesn't care, I suppose, what your excuses are. If you carry those ghosts into your home, you risk unleashing them on your children.

All this means that Celeste and I are building a home from scratch. We don't have blueprints for a reliable foundation. We hadn't learned as children the stories and traditions that are supposed to give life to our new homes. Neither of us knew much, when we had our first child, about how to make a home. We only knew the things we didn't want to let happen. Much of our effort at staying married and being good parents has been the struggle of protecting our children from the ghosts of our own childhoods.

We weren't thinking about ghosts, and the meaning of home, when we started our family. We were a thousand miles from where we grew up, we had a new baby girl, we were living new lives. We had yet to learn the things I am going to tell you. We didn't understand that, however much he may love us, God allows his children to be wounded. We didn't yet see that *home* is a sacred place, and sacred places must sometimes be sanctified by the heart's own suffering.

Most important, we hadn't yet discovered that beyond these stony truths, grace abounds. A home, we are learning even now, can be built in spite of all that our ghosts and the world itself do to try to stop us. That is what we strive for, and perhaps what you strive for as well.

We named our daughter Caroline. She had curly dark hair and chocolate brown eyes. As she learned to talk she spoke with a lilting pixie's voice that carried the faintest trace of southern belle. Like other first-time parents, we had no idea, until we held her, how fiercely you can love a child. It's a feeling that sneaks up on you until one day you find that your heart has become an overflowing cup. This is why new parents gear up like sherpas for a simple trip to the grocery store, and why they make baby talk without regard to who may be listening. It's why they come running at the first peep from their darling infant who, to the rest of us, looks a bit like Winston Churchill: because they have been seized by this desperate set of emotions. This is another way of saying that they have lost their minds.

Additional children don't lessen your love, but they help return some rationality to your outlook. Slowly you learn that babies pooch out their bottom lips and make that mournful wail because they are little psychoanalysts and have determined that you bring the milk much faster when they imitate a broken-hearted kitten. When you are in the throes of love with that first baby, however, all reason goes out the window. We had fallen into irrational love—which is the only kind worth having, if you think about it—with our daughter. We were determined to give her a better home than we had known. She became our chirping shadow and gentle-hearted helper as we tried to create a real home. Life in those first years was dreamlike in its goodness and grace.

Celeste and I came to faith as adults, two years after Caroline was born. On some days I can define what that means with a theological precision that would force even Jean Calvin to proffer a grim smile. Other days, I am that desperate father of a hell-haunted child, whose plea to Christ was recorded by Saint Mark: "If you can do anything, take pity on us."

"*If* you can?" Christ chided, already knowing that soon this father would embrace his healed and whole son. "All things are possible to him who believes."

I've heard plenty of sermons on Bible verses, but never a sermon on what this father replied to Christ, which gives me goosebumps whenever I read it: "I do believe; help my unbelief."

I am that father. There are truckloads of books on the subject of what it means to be a Christian, but for me, it is this desperation, this yearning to find our way even in the midst of hopelessness. *I do believe; help my unbelief.*

There was no burst of light, no voice of God whispering in our ears, but 1998 marks the point when Celeste and I became Christians nonetheless, because it is the year we went from a vague belief in God's existence to the fearful, hope-filled conviction that God knows our names. This is all the difference in the world, between the God who is a kind but remote grandfather in the sky, and Immanuel — *God with us.* We fell into a belief — and this is the only accurate way to describe it — in the Immanuel God. We came to believe that without his grace even faith is impossible. *I do believe; help my unbelief.*

Many people who arrive at faith as adults will tell you that it is an exhilarating time. You have a newfound sense of purpose, and rootedness, and hope. Coming as it did in the midst of our striving to create a home, to be a peace-filled family with good traditions — like pancakes on Saturday mornings and Thanksgivings where you dress up for the meal — we felt like God had gazed down on our meager efforts and chosen to bless us.

As all dutiful new Christians do, we learned our Bible verses — even Caroline learned several — and immersed ourselves in the life of our church. My wife joined a women's group that met to discuss Jesus books, as I thought of them. I joined a men's prayer group, which was a doubly big step for me because it involved sharing emotions with others and getting up once a week at the crack of dawn—and I excel at neither. We thought we had God's protection, not yet understanding what that does—and does *not*—mean.

One cool autumn afternoon, when the leaves had begun to fall with abandon, Caroline came downstairs. Her face was sad and haunted. "I'm going to die," she said. Celeste still shivers when she recounts the matter-of-factness in Caroline's voice. We began to feel the haunting as well. We tried to keep it from our minds. We redoubled our prayers. But in the night's darkness we could sense it. "I feel like something bad is going to happen," I told the men in my prayer group. They were all older and wiser, their walks with God longer. They prayed with me, but none of them told me everything would be all right.

They understood what we had yet to learn, which is that God doesn't always protect us. We are tempted to think that he should be devoted to our earthly happiness. But God has deeper purposes, I think, and inscrutable ways. Sometimes God protects us. Sometimes he breaks us.

It was soon after she turned three that we realized Caroline was sick. She became prone to crying spells, and she began to sleep late into the mornings. She complained of headaches. We only put these symptoms together in retrospect. What led us to take her to the doctor was something else entirely. It was the early summer of 1999, and we had decided to watch a video of our previous summer's vacation. "Oh my God," my wife whispered as we watched our daughter on the television screen. "She talked more clearly then than she does now."

It was a brain tumor. The doctors said it was the size of an egg, lodged on her brainstem. We took her to Chicago

Children's Hospital, and after three horrible days at the hands of the indifferent residents who passed for medical professionals there, we learned they couldn't help her. A surgeon at Johns Hopkins confirmed the prognosis. That tumor wasn't coming out. "It's like someone threw sand into Jell-O," he explained.

We brought our daughter home to die. I couldn't bear to leave her alone in the dark of her room at night, so we put her in our bed. She became like a seam holding us together. In the mornings she would wake us, cheerful and voraciously hungry, a side effect of the steroid that reduced her brain's swelling. "Daddy," she would say, "I want some grits, and eggs, and toast, and apples, and pancakes." Her body wiggled with anticipation. We fed her whatever she wanted, and played games with her, and read to her. We prayed, and we waited.

We started her on chemotherapy as well, and it poisoned everything but that egg-shaped tumor. We watched her hair fall out and her body swell from the steroid. The light began to leave her eyes. It became harder for her to talk.

In the midst of it, we learned that Celeste was pregnant, with a boy. We felt guilty anticipating him, knowing Caroline would probably never see her brother. We told her about him, and asked what she wanted to name him. "Stephen," she said, as if it were a stupid question. Stephen is the name of our pastor's son, with whom she was smitten. Stephen. Of course.

A few days later, Caroline lost her ability to talk. Sometimes, in the weeks that followed, she would reach out a tentative hand and stroke her mother's belly. His name would be Stephen.

We learned how to operate an I.V., how to change out oxygen tanks, and how to administer painkillers to a three-year-old. I kept a diary of the medications. There was Decadron, the steroid that made her flesh balloon. This necessitated Zantac, because Decadron can wear holes in the stomach. Benadryl, we learned, could serve as a first line of defense against pain. Soon she needed Morphine as well.

I still have that medicine diary in my dresser drawer. Sometimes, when I think my paltry troubles are overwhelming, I dig it out and thumb through it. One of the worst days reads:

Benadryl (2:35 a.m.)
Morphine (6:40 a.m.)
Morphine (7:40 a.m.)
Decadron (9:15 a.m.)
Zantac (9:25 a.m.)
Morphine (9:50 a.m.)
Morphine (10:45 a.m.)
Morphine (11:00 a.m.)
Morphine (12:15 p.m.)
Benadryl (12:55 p.m.)
Morphine (1:35 p.m.)
Morphine (2:20 p.m.)
Morphine (2:55 p.m.)
Morphine (4:20 p.m.)
Morphine (5:35 p.m.)
Morphine (6:35 p.m.)
Decadron (7:50 p.m.)

We were lucky that evening, because she passed out from exhaustion, which meant we could eat and shower and sleep. The pain resumed at 4:45 a.m. the next morning. Our days were framed by her suffering.

As Caroline's pain got worse, I nearly killed her with the Morphine. I remember lying beside her, as her breath shallowed to nearly nothing, and praying that I hadn't murdered my daughter. In the weeks that followed, I would agonize over the notion that killing her might be best. I told myself I was waiting on a miracle, but the truth is that I just didn't have the courage to end her suffering. I knew there was to be no miracle. Some days I prayed that she would live just a little longer, and other days I prayed she would die soon. Both prayers made me feel dirty.

Some days Caroline would cry for hours, and we began to worry that it was not only pain, but hunger. Her doctor implied that it would be best to let her starve, but I couldn't do it. I hurried to the store, afraid she might die while I was away, and bought cans of a protein drink. I sat with her propped between my legs and tilted sips of it between her clenched teeth. Most of it spilled onto the folded paper towel I held beneath the cup, but some made its way down her throat. Feeding her this way took five or six hours a day. We couldn't let her starve.

Between the feedings, the medications, the cleanings, and trying to communicate with our daughter who could no longer speak or move, Celeste and I were consumed. People from church brought us meals, did our laundry, and mowed our grass. There were more people who wanted to help than there was work. Only in later years did I learn how rare such a church is.

I was certain there would be no miracle, and Celeste was equally certain one was coming. Often we cared for Caroline in shifts; it was during one of these evenings that I woke from a nap in the spare bedroom and felt the chill of fear settle into my stomach. This was always what waking was like during those months, but now there was a silence in the house that set me on edge.

I hurried to our bedroom. Caroline lay peacefully, for once, on the bed. She was watching her mother with something like curiosity. Celeste was gently washing her. I watched, too, as Celeste swirled a soft cloth in warm soapy water, and then tenderly ran it along Caroline's skin. After she washed a part of Caroline's body, she would stop and pray for it. She prayed that it would not hurt, that it would be life-filled. She prayed over Caroline's toes, her knees, her arms, her tired, sweat-soaked head. The best her prayers could accomplish was a temporary peace, but even this was a miracle.

A few days later, Caroline remained asleep as the morning light warmed our bed. The hospice nurse told us the end would get here soon. A friend said that perhaps Caroline was holding on because she needed permission to leave us, so later that morning I curled close to her in bed, and whispered that it was all right to go. I told her what I imagined heaven would be like. I said that Jesus was coming, that he would take her home. *I do believe; help my unbelief.*

That night, Caroline tried to wake. She stirred, and her breaths began to ease out at odd intervals. Celeste wept, and pulled our daughter onto her lap. Caroline took in a deeper breath, and sighed. She did it again. "This is it," Celeste cried. "She's dying, isn't she?" I leaned close to Caroline's face. Her eyelids fluttered. She was struggling to wake. "Go with Jesus," I told her. "Mommy and Daddy will be there soon."

She sighed once more. She didn't breathe again.

It's strange, how the rules of grammar require me to speak of our daughter as past, because Caroline is very much in our present. The rooms in our home today are haunted not just by our separate pasts, Celeste's and mine, but by the giggles and cries of that little girl. The Portuguese have a word for what Caroline became to us: *saudade*. It means: "the presence of absence."

When you lose someone so close to your heart and flesh, there is an adrenaline rush that helps you get through planning the funeral and receiving well-wishers and helping people cry things out with you. I remember giving Caroline's eulogy, her white coffin stretched in front of me so big and terribly small at the same time, and thinking: *I can do this*. A man I had worked with years before, who had lost his only child when he was younger, heard through the grapevine about our loss. He sent a card with a single word written inside: *Endure*. That's what I was telling myself, that I could endure this. It's what the adrenaline does for you; it helps you bury your child and see everything for a brief time in an elevated spiritual realm. I was serene, and I reflected on the passage in the Bible about the peace that surpasseth all understanding. *The Lord has a plan*, I reminded myself, and *all things work together for good, to those who love God*, which is what the Bible insists.

What they don't tell you, the well-intentioned people who quote Bible verses, is that God never promised everything will work out okay in your lifetime, and that each trouble you face will yield a blessing out of all proportion to the pain. Oswald Chambers wrote that God doesn't promise deliverance *from* trouble; he promises deliverance *in* trouble. It's a subtle distinction that carries all the weight of a dying world.

After Caroline died, Celeste's doctor put her on bed rest, because she was having too many pre-term contractions. She was confined almost nonstop to the bed where our daughter died. With no vacation or sick days remaining, I returned to work. Our bed felt like a refuge when I returned home each evening. I would lie in it, bury myself in the pillows, and breathe deep in hopes of smelling Caroline. It must have been very different for Celeste, to sit there hour after hour, remembering the cries, the last breath.

It was the women from our church who saw Celeste through those darkest months, even as I told myself I was being strong for her. She cried almost hourly, and I responded by crying less and less. I went dutifully to work each morning. I held Celeste as she cried each night. I stifled any feeling that threatened to draw me into the darkness gathering beneath the surface of my skin. I'm being strong, I told myself. The truth is that it was Celeste who was strong; in the end it was me who broke.

Four months after Caroline died, her little brother, Stephen Caleb, was born. I didn't want to hold him. I didn't want to love another child. I was starting to crack, the way thick ice does, in streaks and crevices beneath the surface.

This is the thing about Caleb, and about all of my children: they are to me like grace itself. They creep into my heart through the cracks, just as grace must seep into lost souls. They fill the hollow places. Caleb became, as he learned to walk and talk, what Caroline had been before him — my shadow. Life slowly became something like good again.

Celeste seemed to have coped, as we approached the anniversary of that wretched night, with Caroline's death. I told myself I'd succeeded in being the strong husband. Things were going to get back to where they had been. It wouldn't be the same, it would never be the same, but things would be good. This is what I told myself.

I stayed busy with work, and with being a father again, but this was the ugly thought creeping to the front of my mind: *God killed my child.* I sat in church, and listened to sermons about the power of God, about his kindness. I seethed as I listened to the hymns. He let her die. It was the same as killing her. *God killed my daughter.*

Two years after Caroline died, and just as I was beginning to spiral completely into depression, I met a man who had recently buried his baby daughter, also dead from a brain tumor. "I wish I knew where to find God," he growled, "so I could kill him." This is the anger, and they don't tell you about it in church. Looking into his furious eyes, I saw my own, perhaps for the first time. Everything I'd kept buried — because that's what strong fathers and good Christians do — oozed to the surface. That night I crawled into a bottle of scotch and began the downward slide in earnest.

I want to gloss over what I'm about to tell you because it fills me with shame; but it's also part of the miracle. In the end, this is a story of a home that survives, in spite of ghosts and sins. There is grace after sin, I tell myself. There has to be grace, or else who would stand? *I do believe; help my unbelief.*

Since God seemed unavailable to receive my anger, I unleashed it on my wife. I never used my fists, but words can do plenty of damage on their own. Yes, words can do just fine. She endured it. I think we both believed it was simply a season that would pass. Perhaps as an act of healing, or hope, we chose to conceive another child in that dying bed. Timothy Eli was born two years after his brother, three years after his sister left us.

Eli was the mildest of babies, and it was good to see Caleb with him. Neither of them, however, could fix what was broken. I pulled farther away from Celeste, and she began to show signs of the strain. It became easier to make her cry. I figured her tears were her own fault. I decided I didn't love her, nor she me. My heart grew calloused toward my wife and children, making it easy to seek adoration from other women. I began to cheat on my wife in partial ways, and then altogether—in body, in heart. I blamed her for what I did.

I'm tempted even now to imply that it wasn't my fault, that I was enticed, that I was sick with grief. The truth is that I have always sought admiration from women. Now, with no sense of God or love to restrain me, I simply pursued my nature. I decided I was in love with another woman. I made plans to abandon my family for the fantasy of a perfect life with someone who loved me for all my mysteries and eccentricities. When I was young, I had been Celeste's hero, rescuing her from an abusive home. I was the man she trusted when everyone else abandoned her. Now I was the one betraying her, the one rending her heart.

The first miracle is that I didn't follow through with my plans to leave. The second miracle is that Celeste, after I confessed, didn't beat me senseless with a frying pan and throw me out herself, which is what I deserved. I remember, in the awful weeks and months that followed, how much she cried, and how much it was like a return to mourning our daughter. The first tragedy to assail our home had come from a broken world, or God, or both. The second had come from my own hand.

I was falling into a pit—no faith in God, my wife devastated, my job neglected, and my two sons rapidly becoming emotional wrecks in spite of attempts to shield them from our storm. I saw preachers and psychiatrists. I continued to cheat on her, even as I tried to convince her that I was reforming, that her intuition otherwise was just her own unforgiving nature. I even convinced our friends who knew some of the story that it was Celeste who was impeding reconciliation. I hated myself for it, yet the only solace I could find was to crawl into some other woman's bed. Looking back on that time, I understand a little better how people who have given themselves over to drugs or alcohol or violence can despise themselves for living that way, yet still return to their depravity again and again. I was the dog who returns to his own vomit. I was worse than a dog, because a dog doesn't know any better. I knew better. God forgive me.

On occasion during this dark time I would pray to the *saudade Deus*, as I thought of him—the absent God. I would pray a half-hearted prayer and receive no answer, and so then I would curse and rave and demand that he respond to me. Sometimes in the evenings, as I drove home on dark country roads, I would scream at the top of my lungs until I was hoarse. It felt good, the screaming and the pain. I considered putting a gun in my mouth, but I was afraid I would go to hell, where I would never see my children again.

At my lowest point, as I wept over all I had done and all that was taken, Celeste cried with me. She said she forgave me, but it wasn't enough. There was this cold place inside, this absent God. *Saudade Deus.* "Where is he?" I cried to her. "How will he ever forgive me?"

She held my face in her hands. "Ask him," she whispered.

I didn't want to ask him. What if he didn't answer in this, the moment when I was certain that I was going to kill myself, regardless of what it did to them, regardless of what comes after? How would I bear the silence? No silent God was going to forgive me for what I had done, for what I was still in the midst of doing.

"Ask him," Celeste said again. She has always been the one who believes in miracles.

So I did. I shut my aching eyes and asked God how he could ever open the gates of heaven for the likes of me. Have you ever wondered why this God they talk about in church, who wanders across the pages of your Bible uttering the most outrageous things about justice, about guilt, about mercy, should ever want anything to do with any of us? This is what went through my mind as I prayed my faithless little prayer. *How can you ever forgive me?*

There was no reply—no voice, no vision, no clap of thunder. I began to weep at this death of my last hope. Then they came to me, each an unbidden image, what I never expected— though I should have known all along what his answer would be, has always been. I saw the faces of my children.

Would you ever cast them from your home? This is what the wordless *saudade Deus* offered that night. *I love you, just as you love them.* It's not the miracle I wanted, coming five years after Caroline breathed her last. But miracles are not something I understand.

It's shocking, looking through the journals where I penned

so many of the stories about our family, to see a juxtaposition of despair and grace. On one page I find myself bemoaning how God has gone silent just when I need him, and on the next there is a story about how Caleb and Eli dressed up like knights and chased me around the house with little rubber swords that actually sting *a lot* when you get whacked with one. I see that on the same day I cried out to God in abandonment, I later wrote about lying on the couch with two-year-old Eli, while he whispered his little-boy dreams and plans to me. Looking at these scribblings side by side, I see plainly what was hidden then, which is the fact that when I thought he was absent, God was speaking to me every day. He doesn't always pronounce judgment in a King James voice, you know. Sometimes God is in the whisper of a little boy.

Like I said earlier, grace abounds, even in sorrow. It is in the giggle of a child who doesn't yet know what the world can do. It is in the forgiving touch of a wounded wife. It is in the smell, even, of a dress hanging forgotten in a dead child's closet. It is in the wordless answer to a faithless prayer. Grace abounds in our home, in spite of the ghosts, in spite of me. This is how I have learned that home is also this: *the place that makes us better than we could ever be alone.*

There is something sacred in us, something that draws us to a holy place. This is, I think, the yearning that each of us feels for a home that is something more than the place where we sleep. We all long for home, even as we fill up our days with distractions and strive for success or simply a deadening of whatever pain we're carrying. We may forget for a time that we are homebound creatures, but as we get older we begin to hear the call, many of us, that we heard as children, a voice or whisper or instinct that draws us homeward. I understand, I think, why Christians in the South, where I grew up, say of a dead church member that he or she has "gone home to glory." I believe heaven is a real place, and I believe many of us get through the front door even though we don't deserve it. Just like home.

In the days when community was richer and faith was deeper, a new home would be blessed and its doorsills anointed with oil, or honey, or blood. Before the explosion of churches, some homes even had altars. The first temple, in fact, was called the *Mishkan*: a place of divine dwelling. In English we call it a *tabernacle*: a tent. The first church in the Abrahamic faiths, in other words, was a home. God chose to live among his people. *Home*, in this earlier understanding, was more than a venue for eating and sleeping; it was a holy place.

Somewhere along the way we forgot this. We began to think that God was out there—in heaven, a sunset, an ornate temple, a megachurch. We forgot that he has always come to where we are, to dwell with us. We began to think of him as being somewhere else, and told ourselves that we had to get dressed up, put on smiles, and go out to find him. We forgot that home was meant to be a sacred place because *we* were meant to be sacred.

We have made the home a luxury living and playing space, and forsaken some of the sacred in our lives. In the midst of greater comfort, we complain that we don't eat meals together as often as we should, and that our children are lured by distractions—computers, television, telephones—away from the family, and into their separate rooms. Perhaps part of the reason is that we have outsourced sacredness to our churches, and in so doing we have relinquished the sanctifying power of the home. We have forsaken much of what binds us to God. The altars and anointed doorways are gone, and now we must search for him in the shadows and corners.

Yes, we can go to our churches and temples to seek him out, but I wonder sometimes if our homes are not just as sacred as these buildings. It is our homes where we make love and pray, where we make children and try to raise them, where — if we are blessed — we one day are allowed to die. If God is not in such a place, in the muck of our daily existence, in our beginnings and endings, then he is nowhere.

We used to understand that home is sacred ground, and a place of sanctification. We understood that it is where the sacred and the mundane meet, which is to say, where the hand of God touches the broken heart of man. We used to know these things, and so we labored and we bled to build our homes, and to protect them.

Perhaps, had Celeste and I not watched our child die in our home, and not started our family anew in the same bed where she died, and not wept and fought against the darkness to save it, then *home* might mean no more to us than it does to a realtor. But our home is where we have chosen to stake our ground in the world, to try to build something that we've never known but which we need to believe can exist. This is where we have striven with God, been wounded by God, cried out to God. This is where we seek him daily, sometimes hourly. If he is not here, and in your home, and in the homes of your neighbors, then where will he be found?

Perhaps the reason so many of us have come to feel dis-connected and lost is because we have been thinking of God as being *out there*. Celeste and I believe that God is *here*—in our home, in your home—where his children dwell. Other people can search for him in rigid theologies, in philosophies, in the mysteries of the world or the wonders of their own minds. We will seek him *here*, because a God who lives with his children is the only god who can heal the wounds this world inflicts.

That's part of the reason I tell you the things I've revealed so far, and why I'm going to tell you more secrets, so you will also see more clearly that the home is a sacred place, and that in it you can be sanctified, and made into something better.

This book is the story of how we reclaim the things that are lost. It's also the story of how a home can become sacred, and how in the process it can sanctify us as well. I can tell you these things because I have been in dark places—which is the only way any of us ever learns to love the light. I know what it is to do shameful things, and to have the front door opened to me in spite of them. Home is more than a place where we eat and sleep; it is where we learn grace, where we glimpse heaven. It is where we find or lose God, or perhaps where he finds us if we will only be still long enough to listen for him.

I wander from room to room
like a man in a museum:
wife, children, books, flowers,
melon. Such still air. Soon
the mid-morning breeze will float in
like tepid water, then hot.
How do I start this day,
I who am unsure
of how my life has happened
or how to proceed
amid this warm and steady sweetness?

Albert Garcia, excerpted from "August Morning"

1

The Ring

living room

It's funny how in naming rooms we assign them aspirations. To me, "living room" evokes the image of grand, purposeful activity. *We're really living now,* someone might say in such a place. *Live it up, boys!* the master of the house might tell his companions when they gather in his living room, perhaps while sporting bowler hats and smoking fat cigars.

Likewise do we label "dining room" that place where many children shove macaronis onto their canine teeth and pretend they are noodle monsters. And we euphemistically call "bathroom" that place where mostly we pee and primp. In much the same way "living room" is mislabeled in our home. We might more accurately call it a "wallowing room," or a "secret-place-to-eat-a-cookie-when-Mom-isn't-looking-room," or a "wrestling ring."

Sometimes my sons affect a civilized streak, and use the living room as a place to read. Then our hearts are warmed, Celeste's and mine, because our living room is filled with bookshelves, and we've always hoped that one day we might actually get to read some of the books they hold. We don't really care if we never get to live it up in our "living room";

we'd settle for quietly soaking up words in our "reading room," free of complaints and wrestling and incessant requests for snacks, assistance finding lost toys, justice against a brother who has whacked his sibling, help wiping a behind, and so on. If all our children become gentle readers, we will be very satisfied parents. So we love the sight of a child holding a book in our reading/living/don't-you-dare-break-Mom's-antique-lamp room.

As is perhaps true of all civilizations, however, barbarity is never far from the border. This is the case as I wander into our living room and am initially warmed to spy Eli hunched over a Dr. Seuss book. His blond hair—he and his mother are the only ones in our family with hair that doesn't look like it's in a constant state of rebellion—gleams golden in the sunlight, and I can see his delicate freckles from the doorway. He is so sweet, and quiet, and terribly unaware that four-year-old Isaac—hair all atangle and a hunter's gleam in his brown eyes—has climbed onto the arm of the couch behind Eli, preparing to use it as a turnbuckle from which to administer a devastating tackle.

The key in such a moment is to remember that this instinct of Isaac's will come in handy should he ever become a Navy SEAL, or need assistance in one of those retail establishments that employ teenagers who must have an arm twisted behind their backs before they'll actually help a customer. At the same time, a conscious Eli is much more enjoyable than a bleeding, unconscious one. And there is the deductible for the emergency room visit to consider.

All this goes through my head as I sweep in even quieter than Isaac, who is just now rearing back to give himself extra momentum. As he launches himself I catch him in midair. He cackles with delight because this means Wrestle Time with Dad. I heft him over my shoulder and carry him to a safe place for pretend pile drivers. Eli gazes at us with his chocolate brown doe eyes before returning to his book, oblivious to how close he came to getting clobbered.

I suppose we all have those moments. We often think God stingy because we don't see all the times he protects us from something terrible. We only keep count of the times something bad happens, or something really, really good (as opposed to the good things most of us take for granted, like food and a warm bed and the expectation that our children will outlive us). I suspect that frequently I am like Eli, peacefully going about my business while above me God is striking down robbers, redirecting meteors, and quenching fires before they start.

We parents would protect our children, if we had the power, from every bad thing. This is why some of us have trouble forgiving God after something terrible happens. We stand mourning by that grave where our beloved lies, or we grieve over a spouse who has abandoned us, or we sit in our cold new wheelchair, and we cry out to the God who told us to think of him as a father: *Where were you? How could you?*

We ask these accusatory questions because we believe God has the power to protect us and those we love. He has promised to be a good parent. Yet sometimes he is still when we desperately want him to move. He is quiet when we cry out. Loving parents would prevent every bad thing if they could, but even the best parents sometimes fail their children. Yet God doesn't have that excuse, does he?

God need never fail us, yet it seems that he does.

Some strains of faith try to shrug off this bleak reality by claiming that God really isn't that powerful after all. Bad things happen to good people, they say, because God isn't really omnipotent. Others redefine terms, so that *bad* is actually *good* in some cosmic sense. *All things work together for good*, they'll quote you from the Bible, as if everything that transpires is therefore good. These are often the people who have not buried their children. Most of them have not watched a beloved husband or wife wither away in agony, or received a call in the night that says: *the person you loved most is gone.* They've not stood on a beach where thousands of bloated corpses batter the shore after a tsunami and declared it good, or seen the body of a toddler beaten to death by his own mother and announced that it is according to God's eternal plan.

This Americanized interpretation of the Bible fits our sitcom view of the world, in which all things must be neatly resolved before the episode's end. But Jesus wept over the dead body of his friend even as he intended to restore his life. Suffering and death are heartbreaking tragedies in God's creation, and as he weeps, so do we rightly weep. *All things work together for good* is our hope for the future, when Christ brings us into that place where there "shall be no more death, nor sorrow, nor crying." It is a declaration of God's power to restore all that is being torn asunder, and to bring about the redemption of creation even out of the terrible horrors that darkness unleashes on it.

In the immediate pain of loss, however, that half-verse— *All things work together for good*—is an abstraction at best.

At its worst it is, in the dark night of your soul, an obscenity. This is because we want to believe, even many of us who claim not to believe in God at all, that he is a loving father who will rush to the place where we are imperiled and rescue us from being clobbered.

But sometimes he does not come, and after the casket is placed in the ground, or the divorce is finalized, or the wheelchair is fitted to our useless limbs, we begin to resent him. *Where were you?* we cry out. *Where are you now?* We may pray this to him, or scream it as we drive along a dark country road, or whisper it in the shadows of our minds, terrified to consider what it entails. We may ask it in faithlessness, the way a betrayed spouse might question the one she wants to love but can no longer trust, or in faith, as a wounded child who simply wants to understand. When we suffer all of us ask God the same question: *Why?*

Eventually we hear an answer. It is not the answer we want, but it is better than the silence. That answer, which comes to us while the choir sings in church, or when we lay in the bitter afterglow of weeping, or perhaps simply as we sit quietly over a cup of coffee, goes something like this: *I have been here all along.* It explains nothing. It offers no excuse, no big picture into which our wounds fit nicely. It merely offers up its own wounds, and whispers: *This is what the world does to us. Rest here in me, Beloved, who grieves with you even as others forget your suffering. One day I will restore what was lost, and your face will forget the feel of tears.*

This is the comfort of God within the ashes of your despair. In one sense it is not enough, because we want to know why the all-powerful God who claims to love us did not

dash in to prevent our catastrophe. Often the answer is simply: *It is not for you to know.* This is a hard answer, but sometimes it is the only answer, and so we take solace in knowing
that God grieves with us. When he does not stop us from
being wounded, he receives the wounds as well, just as you or
I suffer when our own children suffer. There is some solace in
that—and in knowing that one day, when the dead rise up
and we no longer see "through a glass darkly," when presumably the answers are finally available, we'll be so happy that
we'll forget we ever had questions.

Sometimes flowers, meanwhile, spring up from those
ashes. We have four of them in our house, though perhaps
"flower" isn't the right word to apply to a child who thinks it
is fashionable to wear nothing but tighty-whiteys and cowboy
boots, sporting a toy sword in one hand and a cap gun in the
other. You think you are settled and dignified, seated comfortably in your living room with a book in your hand, and
then that sight goes traipsing past at the edge of your vision,
and you want to laugh at him except for the fact that he is so
very serious about his accoutrements and you need to take
him seriously too.

No, boys don't frequently resemble flowers, I suppose.
Flowers, after all, enjoy a good shower, but mine argue bitterly
when you tell them it's bath time. Yet in a way I think they are
very much like flowers, and you can see it in how they swell
up with happiness when you love them, as if your words and
touches are rain. They spring up in this home that we thought
would forever feel barren, and they are beautiful to see. Just

don't mention I called them flowers. One day when they have their own children I'll let them read this, and then perhaps they'll understand what I meant.

I suppose boys don't want to be compared to flowers because they want to be made of tougher stuff. At various times they come to you and announce that they want to be knights when they grow up, or cowboys, or Army men. Six-year-old Eli told me recently that he wants to be a knight-fireman. "You want to be a fireman-knight, huh?" I responded, humoring him. "No," he replied. "A knight-fireman." I'm not sure what the difference is, but I told him I can't wait to see the uniform. Eight-year-old Caleb lately talks of becoming a detective, which in his formulation involves a combination of invisible ink and machine guns. I assume without asking that Isaac will forge a career in professional wrestling.

One of the classes Celeste had to endure while earning her Masters in Education from the University of Michigan was ostensibly about differences between boys and girls, though the professor believed there are none. This professor was bent on convincing her students that all differences between boys and girls are "socially constructed," meaning that if not for our sexist behaviors as a society, lots of boys would want to diaper baby dolls, and lots of girls would ask their fathers (or mothers) to show them how to bow hunt. I don't believe this professor had any children. Perhaps that's a prerequisite to being an expert any more, that one not be distracted from one's theories by the messiness of reality. This probably also explains why none of my wife's education professors had any experience teaching actual, live children.

I am by no means a manly man. I don't know how to

hunt, I've never been in the military, and snakes give me the heebie-jeebies. I get teary every time I see that scene in *Planes, Trains and Automobiles* when Steve Martin comes back to find John Candy sitting alone in a train station on Thanksgiving Day. I got teary just typing that sentence about it. So I don't know where my sons are getting all this "social construction" that conditions them to want to be warriors and heroes, but it isn't from me, and it certainly isn't from television shows, which we don't allow them to watch. Whatever the impetus, they aspire to far greater toughness than they will find in their father.

As I write this, Christmas is approaching, and this snowy evening the boys are assembled on the couch, watching *The Polar Express*. Isaac is clutching his beloved Ducky, a little stuffed animal that he carries everywhere. The movie has reached the scene where the train is barreling across ice, trying to stay ahead of the cracks that threaten to plunge it into freezing dark water. The boys are wide-eyed. Isaac has his legs drawn up to his chest, and he is pressing Ducky to his lips. I sit down on the couch and put my arm around him. "It's just pretend, little buddy," I whisper. "Are you scared?"

He leans into me and puts his head against my chest. He smells like chocolate—which I don't think anybody authorized him to eat—and little-boy sweat. "I not scared," he whispers back. "Ducky scared."

I understand this impulse we have—especially we boys and men—to deny our fear. It's most comically evident in those window decals you sometimes see, the ones that declare: *No Fear.* I can't help but assume the opposite, that a teenaged boy (or a man who hasn't left behind his boyish mentality) puts that sticker in his window precisely because he is scared, because he is terrified, and because he is afraid as well that everyone will smell the fear seeping out of his skin and think him unmanly. So he sticks that decal in his window and juts out his chin and tells himself that all these affectations are proof of manhood.

I don't want my sons to know when I am afraid because I don't want them to worry. I spent too much of my childhood worrying. I took Nancy Reagan's admonitions against drug use seriously, and I was afraid the police would come and arrest all of us because my adoptive father grew marijuana and kept other drugs in the house. I worried when he would drink and turn mean. I worried when my mother lay in the bed crying in the middle of the afternoon, or when the food ran low, or when we had to move because we couldn't pay the rent.

All of this makes me want to keep my children from ever knowing that I worry about getting fired and not being able to pay the bills, about dying and not being there for them, about one of them getting sick, about car wrecks and child-snatchers and financial meltdowns and chemical warfare.

Yet worse than seeing my fear, I suppose, would be for them to struggle through life thinking that men are supposed to be fearless. You can only be fearless when you love nothing. Some ascetics in inward-focused religions achieve this state, as do some psychopaths. It is not the path designed for humanity, however. We were crafted to love others, and we are called to love them more than our own miserable skins. If someone loves himself more than all else, then he is still bound to know fear, but it will be a fear that makes him a coward. He will be someone who won't risk hardship to stand up for what's right, who refuses to forego personal comfort for a cause greater than himself.

Only by loving others more than ourselves can we overcome everyday cowardice. Yet ironically it is when we love others more than ourselves that we truly come to know fear. Everyone reading this who has a child or a spouse or beloved brother or sister knows this fear. It is the fear that they will suffer and be taken from you, and that there is nothing you can do about it. It is the fear that flits across the back of your mind even in good times, like the shadow cast by a lone cloud on a sunny day. It is the fear that forms like ice around your heart when illness strikes, or they have gone missing, or they persist in harming themselves despite all your praying and begging that they not destroy what you love.

My prayer for each of my sons is that one day they will love others more than themselves. In effect I am praying that they will know fear. So if my job is to help prepare them for manhood, I will have to teach them that real men are afraid, and that we go on in spite of it. I will teach them as well that a real man needs a real woman by his side, and real women are afraid too. We are all of us cold with fear sometimes, but because we are truly men and women, and not among the growing crowd of perpetual adolescents brimming over with self-absorption, we press on in spite of our fears.

I used to think that I had to exhibit only strength in front of my boys. I figured they needed someone to show them how to conquer the world. Yet lately I have been thinking about how God approached us when he took on human form. He came not in glory, but in meekness. He came and suffered in our darkened world, declaring all along: *This is how you must live if you would abide in me.*

Many men know what it's like to yearn for someone to show us what it means to be fully a man. We look in vain to our national heroes, to our captains of industry, often to our own fathers. We come to them with a deep, desperate hope that someone will show us how we can become all that men are supposed to be, so that we can finally believe, in the depths of our hidden hearts, that we are not simply pretending. Too often we come to believe that being a man means to rarely cry, to show no fear. Yet look what God did. He came to us where we are, he joined us in our frailty, he wept at suffering, and he felt the grip of fear. He was fully man.

This is what I think when I draw Isaac close beside me on that couch, both of us comforting his Ducky who is scared. I'm pretty sure I overthink things. The future of Isaac's manhood is not hanging in the balance of this moment. But these little ones are so delicate, and I am a fool twice over, not knowing much at all about how to be a man myself, let alone teach boys to do the same. In no single instance will I fail my children irreparably, but if we aren't attentive to these moments when they come, I think we run the risk of falling too far behind in the marathon that is raising a child. I draw Isaac closer, and whisper to him that when I was little — like Ducky — I used to be afraid too. "And sometimes," I tell him, "I still am."

They'll know fear soon enough, these boys. I want them to remember that I knew it too. And I pray that they'll also look back on me walking out of my tiny, backyard Garden of Gethsemane, atop my own little molehill of adversity, with the same prayer on my lips that was uttered by he who was fully man: *Not my will, Father, but thine.*

It's movie Sunday again, and the boys know their rights. They know that on Sundays they get to assemble in our living room and watch a movie. They know further that we are obligated to make popcorn for them, and to serve it up with flavored fizzy water. Nowhere in this unwritten collective bargaining agreement is there anything about candy, but lately they've taken to grumbling like U.A.W. members over an empty cruller tray if there isn't some of that handed out as well.

On movie Sundays they get to pick, and today they want to watch "The Caroline Movie." This is what they call the videotape of our daughter, which has snippets from birthdays and Christmases, as well as wonderfully long and pointless scenes of her playing outside, or singing to her parents in the playroom of our first house. Celeste's grandmother once remarked how nice it was that we had filmed these real moments, and not just special events, and I think she's right. It's the randomly captured parts of our lives that have the greatest power to evoke who we truly are.

My sons are fascinated with this sister they've never met. They want to know what she liked to eat, and what books I would read to her at bedtime. When they hear Isaac mispronounce a word (like "brudder" instead of "brother," or "hink" instead of "think"), they want to know what words Caroline got wrong. This always confuses Isaac a bit, because he doesn't see what's wrong with any of his words. When they are babies we show them her pictures, and teach them to say "sister." For some reason each of our babies has been animated upon seeing his sister's picture, as if some small part of his heart has her name etched upon it, even before he can say "Caroline."

So I distribute the popcorn. Celeste puts in the tape, and it begins playing at the part where people sang "Happy Birthday" at her second birthday party. She is seated in a chair with her eyes wide, and she is watching everyone sing to her. The boys crunch popcorn and watch her, their eyes following her every movement. They laugh when they see Dad trying to be funny. They point out that I didn't have a goatee back then. They repeat her phrases.

I go into the kitchen because I am going to make spaghetti. There are vegetables to cut and even though it is only afternoon you have to start early if you want your sauce to turn out well. There's lots to do here in the kitchen. I go into the kitchen and I turn my back to the door and quietly weep while I pretend to cut vegetables. I listen to my dead daughter's voice and I weep.

Celeste finds me, because you don't bury a child together and not know when the other is grieving. She puts her arms around me. I am reminded once more how much stronger she is than I am, how hope in the world to come runs through the center of her like an iron rod. When I have finished crying she leads me back into the living room. There will be plenty of time later to make spaghetti. We sit down with our boys who miss the sister they haven't met.

I think of this room as a ring because of all the wrestling, but now it occurs to me that it is a different sort of ring. We are gathered close on the couch, and there is Caroline on the television screen, laughing as she stands before the camera, the wind gently blowing her dark curls. In this moment we are all in the same place for a time, a family the way we were supposed to be, and might have been, and are sometimes still, in those rare nighttime hours when I dream about her and she is alive with us on this earth.

The light pouring from the kitchen grows more pronounced as daylight begins to fade, and because we are watching Caroline I think of that night she died. I sat on a couch then too, after they had wheeled her body out on a gurney. Women from church talked quietly in our kitchen. I wept then too, with abandon, as I have never wept before or since. The women in our kitchen fell silent once I began to cry out. There is something sobering, I suppose, about the sound of a grown man weeping like a broken child. Then I began to shiver uncontrollably, and my head felt like it was exploding, and my pastor—a former Eagle Scout—declared that I was in shock. Celeste put a blanket around me and held me that way, much as her arm is around me now. This is how the memories come to you, triggered by a spot of light from the kitchen or the smell of autumn or the sound of a branch tapping against your window.

As we sit on this couch together I remember the time I lounged on it while watching a Saturday afternoon basketball game, heedless of how little time we had left with our daughter. Caroline had flitted between Celeste and me that afternoon, each of us absorbed in something that seemed more important at the time, until she could stand it no longer. She stood in the middle of the living room and burst into tears, saying: "I want someone to play with me!"

So I played with her, but I begrudged her that, because I wanted to see that stupid game, because I worked an irritating job and felt like I deserved some free time, because I was unable to see how the things we love can vanish like breath.

This makes me think of every time I was harsh or impatient with her, and I am so filled with shame that I can barely watch her on the television screen.

"I love these little people," says the narrator in Charles Dickens's *The Old Curiosity Shop*, "and it is not a slight thing when they, who are so fresh from God, love us." It is no slight thing at all, is it? It's also no slight thing that these little ones — perhaps because they are infused, if only for a while, more greatly with the spirit of heaven than the spirit of this world — forgive us everything, even before we ask. *Forgive me, Caroline.* This is what I've asked a thousand times since she died, for all the things I got wrong. Each time I do this I try to remind myself that she forgave everything, and so does God, and that the only person still keeping accounts is me.

It's late, and after much pleading and threatening and a little bribery as well, all of the children have gone to bed. At Christmas I like to lie on the couch with my arms wrapped around Celeste, blankets and our bodies keeping us warm. We hold tight to one another and gaze at the lights. We have Christmas trees in every room, some with big old-fashioned lights of glowing orange, green, red, and blue, some with small white lights that twinkle, some with lights shaped like candies and stars. It's a big production, unpacking all our Christmas gear, and maybe that's part of the satisfaction of lying together in the glow of Christmas.

I suppose as well it's the safety, holding someone you love amidst this feeling of God so close that you can almost hear his voice. At Christmas we celebrate the Incarnation, the coming of God to live with us as a man, shouldering our burdens, enduring with us our trials. Have you ever tried to carry a heavy burden, felt its weight on your shoulder or against your leg, and then suddenly felt it lighten as a friend arrived to help you with it? This is Christmas to us.

As we lie on this couch glowing with lights around us, basking in the presence of the drawn-near God, it occurs to me that I have ignored my daughter on this couch, and held her close just as I now hold Celeste. I have plotted divorce on this couch, and begged forgiveness. I have sat here with my arms stretched wide enough to hold all my family but that one missing girl, and lain here alone in the dark. Grieving, laughing, snoring, wrestling, arguing, holding tight to what we love and desperately fear losing—all these things we've done in this room.

Maybe we're right to call this a *living* room after all.

The world begins at a kitchen table. No matter what, we
must eat to live.
The gifts of earth are brought and prepared, set on the table.
So it has been since creation, and it will go on.
At this table we sing with joy, with sorrow. We pray of suffer-
ing and remorse. We give thanks.
Perhaps the world will end at the kitchen table, while we are
laughing and crying, eating of the last sweet bite.

Joy Harjo, excerpted from
"Perhaps the World Ends Here"

2

Double, Double Toil and Trouble

the table

Boys *eat*. All animals eat, of course, but boy animals are the only creatures to transform eating into a spectator sport. Consider a typical night at our dinner table: There is Caleb, who has wolfed down more mashed potatoes than his father. He is rubbing his pooched-out belly like an expectant mother and making He-man noises. Next to him is Eli, who has quietly but methodically initiated some kind of murky food-science experiment in his water glass. Across from them, Isaac has just fallen out of his chair, a green bean in one hand and a chicken leg in the other. On his way down he's managed to whack his mother with the chicken leg.

And then there's the newest addition to our family, Isaiah John, sitting in his high chair. He has secretly grabbed a biscuit from the table and crammed the entire thing into his mouth while no one was looking. His cheeks are full to bursting. His brothers notice his chipmunk face and begin to giggle. He tries to smile, but his mouth can't stretch because of the biscuit. He claps his hands and hoots back at them, blowing pieces of biscuit onto the table. They laugh harder, making him bob and hoot more enthusiastically. A shower of crumbs bounces like soggy hail across the table. I try to root out some of the doughy mound, but his giggle turns to a squawk of indignation. I settle for persuading him to take a swig from his sippy cup. I'm hoping it will soften the biscuit enough for him to actually swallow some of it before his gag reflex kicks in and we get chain-reaction upchucking.

In these moments my poor wife looks at me as if for an explanation, like I am a spokesman for the entire male species. She is waiting for an excuse. She hasn't yet learned that we men rarely have an excuse. I can't help but think that perhaps this is an additional curse laid upon women, that they have to sit at a dinner table with us. Eve did eat that forbidden piece of fruit, after all. It's a poetic kind of punishment, if you think about it.

One thing I've learned in marriage, however, is that you ought not voice every idea that floats into your head. Celeste probably wouldn't agree that poetry best describes what goes on at our dinner table. And neither of us can help but think that there must be lots of families with small children who still manage to eat dinner like civilized human beings.

Not that sitting at a dinner table together is a tradition that one can take for granted any more. We have a multitude of activities to draw us away from our families these days. What's more, in this digital age many houses have become personal entertainment complexes rather than family homes. Televisions in every room, each family member with a computer and Internet access, and likely a cell phone as well, all implements designed to pull our attention away from one another and toward people and things outside our home.

Food companies have obliged our distractions by giving us

every manner of portable, individual meals. Now Dad can eat a pizza and gawk at Monday Night Football on his widescreen TV, Jimmy can surf the Web while scarfing down a microwave burrito, Susie can text-message to her heart's content as she gulps a health shake, and Mom can sit alone at the kitchen table and read a romance novel while munching a pre-made salad. If you tried to pass a law prohibiting Americans from eating together as families, most of us would fetch our guns. But offer us discount coupons for TiVo and microwaveable chicken wings in three tasty flavors, and too many of us will be happy to let the dust gather on our dinner tables.

It's not just self-oriented distractions that pull us away from the family table. Many of us have longer commutes than our grandparents endured, and more families today have both parents working. We're tired when we get home, and there's a plethora of cheap food available from any number of fast-food joints and restaurants. But have you ever noticed how most of them are geared toward individual meals, not shared dishes that require interaction? And even when families stick together on these eating-out experiences, likely as not we are surrounded by music and a television perched in every corner.

Worse, as our children get older we embrace the entirely modern notion that they need to spend most of their waking hours with others their own age. It's as if we think they are animals we have been keeping all this time, and now that they are approaching adulthood they must be released into the wild to be acclimated to their own kind. So we give them cars and let them work 20, 30, even 40 hours a week while they are in high school. We trust that they can manage the perilous transition to independence without much meaningful contact with their parents. We allow the house to become, for too many teenagers, a hotel rather than the family home.

No, the family dinner is definitely not something to take for granted. But come to think of it, maybe we got to this place precisely because we took it for granted. We began to conceptualize the family as an artifact, or an involuntary designation. You can choose your friends, but not your family, goes the aphorism. It's true in one sense — your parents are your parents regardless of where you go or what you think of them. You can move to the other side of the world and start a new life for yourself, but your brother is still your brother. If you win the lottery, all those relatives who never send you Christmas cards will suddenly show up to claim you as their dear blood relation. If you become president and one of your siblings is a buffoon, you can be certain that everyone will read about his foibles on the front page. It's true, you can't choose your family.

While we can't choose our families in that most basic sense, we choose *what to make of* our families every day. When fathers are rarely home because they are pursuing big bonuses and promotions, when families eat meals in front of the television instead of the table, when parents overbook their children in countless activities and sports, then they are making choices that pull their families apart. "If we do not serve what coheres and endures," writes Wendell Berry, "we serve what disintegrates and destroys." Most people never wake up and decide to disintegrate their families, but we make a series of decisions over the years — most of them seemingly small and harmless and often well-intentioned — that gradually erode the bonds we have been charged as parents to maintain.

I'm not sure when during my boyhood my family stopped eating meals together. To be honest, I can't recall many times that we sat at the same table. I mostly remember eating on the floor in front of the television. When I was older I ate in my bedroom, if I was home at all. Meanwhile we used our dining room table, quite literally, as storage space.

Celeste's home followed a more traditional approach, but it was hollow, because the man at the head of her table was a predator. They also went together to church on Sundays. It's possible to follow the form of things without ever really drawing close to the true heart of how we are supposed to live. We are creatures designed to live in communion with one another and with God, after all. How did we get to this place where we readily forsake the intimacy of breaking bread with those we love?

Sharing a meal is an intimate act. It is set in motion because someone is willing to spend precious time sorting and preparing food for the people she loves. It doesn't have to be one person preparing the meal, of course. We look forward to the day when our boys help, once we can rely on them not to skewer one another with the knives and forks. (This is no small feat in a home of would-be pirates.) But whoever prepares a meal is serving as protector and nourisher, casting aside what the decay of the world has marred, offering her loved ones life. She is crafting more than food to fill our bellies; she is preparing an offering of love. Maybe it's just homemade mac and cheese (our favorite), but it has been given in love, which is why a home-cooked meal always warms the heart as fancy restaurant food never can.

God told his people they could show their love for him by bringing food sacrifices to his tabernacle. Later he took on human form to show his love for us, declaring himself food and drink for his children. *I am the living water*, he promised. *You will thirst no more.* Many Christians still believe, when they come to the communion table, that we are consuming not just bread and wine, but the very body and blood of a Savior. Food can be much more than protein, fat, and carbohydrates. There was once sacredness in these things that we have made small and inconsequential and packaged in bright microwaveable wrappers.

So the preparer of a meal sets it before those she loves, and then if the father has an ounce of faith he pronounces a blessing over it. If it's a mother caring for her children alone, she likewise blesses the meal, and God smiles on her. It's a flat-out miracle that my marriage has survived so far, and so, in addition to the food, I bless the hands that prepared it, because without them we would be utterly lost, me and my boys. It's her hands that hold us together, that make this house our home. I bless the food and her precious hands and then we open our eyes. We are gathered as a family, each of us facing the others, the food arrayed before us, and we are about to satisfy two of mankind's great hungers—for nourishment and for love. This is intimacy, and the world yearns for it. I think the world also fears it, which explains why we are so easily drawn into isolation and casual, manageable relationships. We yearn to be known, but we fear what people will think when they truly know us.

I used "she" in the cooking example above because in our house as in many, it's poor mom who has almost all the cooking chores. This evolved because, like most working fathers in America, I labor outside the home. Celeste does not, and so the exigencies of time management mean that responsibility for dinner mostly falls on her. Sometimes I cook—big, ambitious, Daddy-type dishes, like lasagna, spaghetti, chili, grilled steaks with homemade mashed potatoes. Sometimes I announce we are going to McDonald's, which is just about the cheapest way I know to make yourself a hero in the eyes of four children. But the daily grind of feeding those youngsters and me falls primarily on Celeste.

In an odd way we know it is an act of love when she does it, because she does not like to cook. She wasn't taught to cook by the women in her family, and her single-track, see-something-to-completion method is ill-suited to meal preparation. I like to tell her that enduring this is part of God's plan for her sanctification. I don't say this when she has a heavy skillet handy or anything else that can be swung with lethal force at my head. She is a good woman, but a person can only take so much of someone else's righteousness, which is probably why many people avoid church.

Sometimes the boys and I will make a "fancy" dinner for her. We'll whip up an elaborate and messy meal, set our table with the good china, light candles, and get dressed up. Then one or more of the boys will lead her into the dining room, staring up at her with expectant smiles, eager to see her delight. And even if her respite has been repeatedly interrupted because I've had to ask where various utensils are hidden, or because the littler ones want to climb all over her while she tries to read, she still smiles and declares how nice it is to have all these men taking care of her. And then we all beam, me included, because in his heart a boy or a man wants very much to take care of a beautiful lady.

I'd like to tell you what follows in our home is graceful dining that would make Miss Manners teary-eyed with approval, but you've already had a glimpse of the circus that frequently sets up tent at our dinner table. I suppose over time we'll get more ordered and mannerly, but here is the point: our lives—and yours—are a continued mingling of the disastrous and the sacred. Who we are is worlds apart from who God is, and that chasm might have remained forever if not for the fact that he came to us *as* we are, *where* we are. We spiritualize and intellectualize this God, who has from the very beginning, come to his people, pursued us, and lived among us, because doing so makes him safely distant, more easily understood. But he comes to us. He comes so that we might become—some more slowly than others and perhaps me slowest of all—like him.

So the meal needn't be elegant, its participants well-versed in etiquette. Every dish doesn't have to be cooked to perfection, or adequately warmed, for that matter. What's important is that we not throw away yet another moment of sacredness in our desperate quest to distract ourselves. These fleeting moments of beauty and joy are all we have to shore ourselves up against the sorrow that inevitably finds anyone who has the courage to bind his heart to another.

In those hours of sorrow we learn that the table which once harbored so much pleasure can become a mourning place. Those who have helped someone die at home know how rapidly that table can be transformed from joyful destination into way station. It is where you come to eat a scrap while the one you love sleeps fitfully upstairs. The food you consume has lost its flavor, and you eat it only because you know you must not collapse before seeing your beloved to the other side. Perhaps you sit at this table in order to cry and pray out of earshot, or to speak with hospice workers, or to receive the awkward good wishes of those brave enough to visit you in this dying house. They often bring food, these well-meaning friends, oblivious to the fact that food has lost its meaning to you, that you don't believe you can ever eat another peaceful meal at this table again.

If you look through the kitchen doorway you can see medicine bottles and canisters, and on the refrigerator the cards and scraps of paper telling you how to contact the doctor, the pharmacist, the medical supply company, perhaps the mortician. Inside the refrigerator are the medications you have to keep cool: the painkillers, the drugs to counteract the poisons administered in vain by the doctors, perhaps a pile of IV bags slouched in a corner where once rested a bowl containing your beloved's favorite soup. You don't look at these things unless you have to because you cannot afford to break down and weep the way you would like, because if you start weeping from the depths of your weariness you might never stop, and any minute now this person you are losing will call out and you will have to go apply a cool cloth to the forehead, a trembling hand to the face, another vial of morphine in the veins.

Your kitchen is where the women will congregate when they finally get the phone call they have been waiting for— and perhaps praying for—a call announcing the departure of a soul. They will stack casseroles in your freezer and talk quietly while they clean your already clean counters and sweep your smooth floor. They will whisper and quietly weep while their husbands stand in corners with hands in their pockets, wishing they were anywhere but here because there is nothing a man hates more than feeling helpless.

They will look up as you enter the kitchen, you who feel as empty now as vain prayers. They will peer into your face like you have the answer to a terrible question. They will look up and some of them will cry, and others will wait for you to cry, and perhaps you will search for the words to explain that you didn't know it would be like this, that in all those nights of waiting for the end you never considered the possibility that along with your broken heart would come relief. You are empty and relieved and so full of shock at watching what death does in those last seconds that you don't have any words. You don't think you will have words ever again.

Later you will sit at this very same table and try not to look at the empty chair while you sort out bills from the doctors and pharmacists and medical suppliers who couldn't help you. Perhaps you will consider the irony in the fact that the only vendor who fully delivered is the man who buried that person you have lost. He has buried a part of you as well, at no additional charge.

I don't remember the first time Celeste and I shared a meal at our table after Caroline was gone. I don't remember much about those months, except the helplessness. Then Caleb came, and as he grew he took the seat that once belonged to his sister. You might expect that would foster resentment in our hearts, but it did not. Caroline named him, after all, when he was still inside her mother. Watching him in her chair pleased us in that bittersweet way all subsequent happiness does after someone you love is taken from you.

We have a picture of Caleb at a year old. He is sitting in my lap, and before him is a plate of cherry pie. He is bug-eyed over the pie. I am temporarily restraining him, for the sake of getting a picture. Soon after that picture was taken, Caleb learned that cherry pie tastes even better than it looks. I can remember laughing and feeling, if not right, then closer to right than I had felt in a long time. I still had a dark path to wander to get to *right*. But I know Caleb — and his brother Eli after him, and Isaac after them — helped heal me.

So our table gradually filled up. Those of you with children know what this is like in the beginning. You prepare a meal, and then you chop it into tiny pieces for the toddlers. You do this not only to keep them from choking, but because you'd prefer to get hit with a small piece of carrot than with the entire carrot. This is how Isaiah John announces that he is finished with his meal. He beans you with something, and then he systematically begins dropping things from his high chair until you clear his tray. He says "uh-oh" before he releases each item, leaning over the armrest of his high chair to observe where it lands. Isaiah has two first-born clean freaks for parents, so he finds this an effective strategy for securing early release from his mealtime prison.

For a while we were afraid something was wrong with Isaiah John. One of his pupils is sometimes bigger than the other, and he was having trouble swallowing. These are symptoms associated with brain tumors. When you have lost a child to disease, you are prone to suspect it in your other children.

Various medical checks and procedures confirmed, however, that there's nothing seriously wrong. "Some eyes just do that," said the ophthalmologist. "His throat is probably just a little narrow," said the radiologist. So we persisted in trying to feed him whole foods, and he persisted in throwing up on us.

One day it was just the two of us in the kitchen, Isaiah John and me. He was irritable because I wasn't providing sufficient entertainment, and I was irritated because I had work to do. We were both a little hungry, and so in a moment of inspiration and desperation I fetched the Cheerios.

These tiny wheels of fun have a long history in our family. Each of our children has learned to count with the assistance of Cheerios. It's a safe bet that when you change a diaper in our house, a Cheerio is going to tumble out of the child's clothing. They are under every couch seat and scattered throughout our minivan. If Cheerios grew on trees we would be living amidst an orchard, given all the Cheerios planted in our carpet.

As I retrieved the Cheerios for Isaiah John, I thought about when Eli was not much older than Isaiah John is now. He was sitting in our kitchen one morning, snuffly from a cold, happily crunching Cheerios. Between the Cheerios and slobber and snot, Eli most definitely did not look like one of those kids you find gracing the cover of a Hanna Andersson catalog. He saw me watching him, and so he toddled over to where I sat. "Kiss?" he whispered. Eli is the quietest of our children. "Kiss?" he asked again, his voice soft but insistent. I leaned over and kissed him on the cheek. "No no no no no," he corrected. "*Kiss.*" He closed his eyes and pooched out his slobbery lips.

Such moments test your love, not to mention your faith in whatever vitamins you've been taking. I considered wiping his face first, but that felt like I would be telling him he wasn't good enough. So I kissed his wet, messy, expectant little lips. "Mmmwaah," he announced. "Good kiss."

And it was.

For some reason this crossed my mind as I offered Isaiah his first Cheerio. He leaned forward, nabbed it with the only two teeth in his head, and worked it around in his mouth. I sat with a paper towel in hand, ready to catch hurl. Isaiah grimaced. He swallowed. No hurl. We stared at each other, both of us surprised that there was no gagging. I cheered. Isaiah cheered. Then he squawked for another Cheerio.

Isaiah John's newfound Cheerio tolerance blossomed into an addiction that continued unabated for three months. If we were in the minivan, he would squawk because he knew we kept a bag of them under his seat. If he was in the kitchen, he would squawk because he could see other people getting food, which reminded him of his precious Cheerios. If he was in the pantry, he would squawk because he could see the beloved box. And if he was at the dinner table, regardless of what was being served, he squawked for Cheerios. It occurred to me that we had taught the boy to do so, by virtue of handing them to him whenever he became intolerable. I had a vision of Isaiah John ending up on a street corner as an adult, holding a sign: "Will squawk for Cheerios."

I said we trained Isaiah John, but in reality I suppose he trained us. Children have a knack for training you without you realizing it. Consider Isaac, for example, who at a year old developed a talent for screeching at the top of his lungs. It was a bloodcurdling scream. When Isaac went on a screaming tear it was like being locked inside the chimpanzee exhibit, only without the prospect of being hit with flying poo, though if he could have wrenched his diaper loose I wouldn't have put it past him.

For the longest time I couldn't figure out why Isaac would scream like that. The boy's got a good life, I reasoned. He has unfettered access to breasts — unlike, say, his father. He sleeps whenever he wants. He is doted on by everyone in the family, not to mention countless women in public places. He can fart with impunity, and even laugh at the sound, and people find it endearing. This is a life most men would envy. So why the bloody screaming?

The answer came to me one Saturday as we sat around the table eating lunch. Isaac barked one of his heart-stopping banshee screams, and without thinking we all made placating *shush* sounds in unison. Isaac grinned with delight at our performance, like he'd been expecting our response. He screeched again. Without looking up from our plates, we all *shushed* again.

He was the conductor, you see, and we were his orchestra.

Parenting is treacherous work. They train us without us realizing it, and often we unintentionally train them as well. Why else would their bad habits and sins so clearly follow our own? If we are judgmental, our children have something negative to say about everything. If we are short-tempered, they fly off the handle at the slightest provocation. If we give up easily, they become quitters too.

We think of training as a deliberate act, as when we instruct them to say "yes ma'am" or show them how to tie their shoes. It's the non-deliberate training to which we should be more attentive. We all have to stand before God for our own sins, but very often we fathers (and mothers) set our children on a path toward suffering by subtly teaching them to fall prey to the wickedness that bedevils us. That's a sobering thought when you consider Christ's warning to those who would lead children into sin.

And I suppose we have to be careful that our children don't lead *us* into sin either, of the yelling-at-them-because-they-won't-shut-their-pieholes variety. Parents with small children know what it's like to attempt a conversation while several chirpy voices try to outtalk you. We discovered this when Caleb, at three, reached a stage of development that I refer to as the Endless Monologue months. It first became apparent one afternoon in our car, when he decided to make up a story. He went on and on, with a host of characters and perils, some drawn from real life, some purloined from who knows what source, some sparking to life in his own fast-firing synapses. The boy talked until he fell asleep.

The next day found us in the car again, which reminded Caleb of his unfinished story, and so he continued his three-year-old's version of *War and Peace* until finally — mercifully — he declared: "And that's the end of my story."

Not that it was the end of the talking, mind you. Just that particular story. He was like Howard Cossell in that car seat, narrating every event. "Red light. Green light. Daddy made Mommy laugh. Black truck. Red light. Oooo ..." his head turning now to linger on the object of his affection, his lips savoring every letter, "Mc — D — o — n — a — l — d — s."

Not only was this child an endless font of speech, he would interrupt your sentence to repeat whichever of your words happened to catch his fancy, like "basketball," or "pancakes," or, of course, "McDonald's." It was as if your saying it and his repeating it might magically cause the blessed object to materialize. Once Caleb went fully verbal, it was like being trailed by a three-foot-tall investigative reporter eager to stop the interview in order to read you chapters from his epic novel. There was a long period of time where every paragraph spoken in our house had some of Caleb's words, somewhere, inserted into it.

At that time, one-year-old Eli couldn't yet compete with his older brother in the word game, but at meal time he would make a loud "Ah-goom" sound with every bite. If you analyzed that sound, you would find that the "Ah" was in anticipation of tasting something yummy, the "g" was an incidental noise emitted as the food went in, and the "oom" was his version of "mmm."

So we are at the breakfast table one Saturday morning when it hits me: *These people are driving me crazy.* Caleb is on one side, chattering about toys and motorcycles and everything else that enters his head. Eli is on the other, stuffing his face and making his *Ah-gooms.* Poor Celeste, meanwhile, is oblivious to the reality that uninterrupted adult conversation has now gone the way of sleeping in on a Saturday morning.

I am trying to be a good husband and listen, because she is deep into planning some remodeling. Planning is, for my wife, a pseudo-interactive exercise best met with what relationship books call "active listening." It works like this: she details her latest thoughts on where, say, the cabinets should go in the utility room, and then I show I've been listening by saying what a good idea that is. But this only works when there is space for all your words. Otherwise you get this:

"I think the cabinets should go ..."

"Ahgoom."

"Dad, did we have pizza the other night?"

"Yes."

" ... that last one once we mud those holes ..."

"Ahgoom. Mmm."

"Dad, is that a circle pancake?"

"Yes."

" ... don't you think that will look good?"

"Ahgoom. Heh heh."

"Pizzas are round like pancakes. So are Cheerios."

"Yes dear."

"For the shelving we'll need ..."

"Ahgooooommmmm."

"I need some syrup on this pancake."

"You have syrup."

"Ahgoom. AHGOOM!"

"This piece doesn't have syrup Dad."

"It's floating in a pool of syrup."

"But I need syrup *on* it."

"Fine."

"We also need to hook up that sink, and I'll need you to cut holes in the back ..."

"EEEEEEWAAAAH!"

"Good Lord, what is wrong with that boy?"

"He's upset because he's done with his pancake. Now I was thinking that the sink should go ..."

"WAAAAHAAAA!"

"Honey, for the love of all that's holy, give him another pancake."

"He's had two."

"Dad, he's already had two. Two pancakes. One, two."

"AAAAAAAHAAAAAA!"

"Three won't hurt. He's a growing ..."

"Excuse me, Dad. Did you say *growing*?"

"Huh? Yes."

"You said he's *growing*?"

"Okay, tubby, Daddy says you can have another pancake. These boys are going to eat us out of house and home one day."

"I ..."

"Excuse me, excuse me, Mom. Did you say *house and home*?"

"Yes, Caleb. What were you going to say honey?"

"I forgot."

"You forgot, Dad?"

"Yeah."

"Heh heh heh. That's so silly, Dad."

For a while I thought I was getting early Alzheimer's, because I kept losing my train of thought at the dinner table. Then I realized there's nothing wrong with me. It's *them*. Sometimes Celeste complains that we never talk. But I feel overloaded with the sheer crushing burden of talk. Maybe I don't talk enough, but there sure are plenty of words packed under our roof. And then there's my day job, with its massive, copious, largely superfluous array of talking to, above, about, around, for, down to, and sometimes even *with* my colleagues and associates. Oh dear Lord, I sometimes pray, I need a day of not talking.

I've heard people say that a parent's relationship with his children is like God's relationship with us. We constantly need correction and guidance, but always he has forgiveness welling up from a deep heart of love that only a parent can begin to fathom. If you want to understand how God can forgive your repeated sins, have children. Yet even with this love comes frustration; one can almost hear it when God says to his children: *Be still, and know that I am God.*

Be still. Be quiet. Even the Almighty God wanted his kids to shut their yaps sometimes. I'm beginning to understand that many of the things my mother did were not, in fact, proofs of mental illness, but merely symptoms of parenthood. Some days we just need a little blessed silence.

I try to remember that the day will come too soon when they have their own children to raise, and then they'll be the ones tangled in endless conversations about handwashing and poop and what is appropriate to carry onto the slide (soccer ball, yes; the cat, no). They'll probably go a little crazy too, and hopefully I'll be there to tell them that, sadly, it doesn't last. And in the quiet I'll miss them and their chatter, and I'll likely respond with joy when they let Grandpa visit and sit at their table and just ... listen.

So when the chaos is causing my face to twitch, I try to think about the fact that a quiet house, while saner, is also a little melancholy. I grit my teeth and remind myself: You will miss this one day. That's probably our miserable lot in life, most of us, to always be thinking of some other time we can't wait to get to, rather than savoring the time we are in. Recognizing this gives us eyes to see the hilarity these little knuckleheads bring into our home.

"Dinner is ready!" Celeste announces in her edgy, I-cooked-for-you-people-while-you-all-conspired-to-drive-me-crazy voice. Isaiah John is squawking because he is equipped with an internal biological alarm that triggers not only when he senses Cheerios, but whenever anyone puts him down. We hear his brothers tromping up the steps to the back door. There is still hope that we might eat dinner while it is warm. Isaac throws open the door, takes one step inside, and looks down to see where that *squish* noise is coming from. He remembers that he has been playing in the creek with only socks on. He dutifully bends over to remove his socks. Eli doesn't expect this sudden halt, however, and so he walks into a bent-over Isaac, who sprawls face-first into the floor. Isaac rolls around on the floor and wails. Eli remembers to close the door for once; if only he had remembered that Caleb's nose was in the line of fire. *Splat.* Wailing from the other side of the door.

Here we are, dinner cooling, seventy-five percent of our children crying, and Celeste beginning to develop that I-need-to-go-out-and-eat-by-myself-and-don't-you-dare-try-to-stop-me look on her face. I am holding Isaiah in one hand, and a bottle of whisky in the other. "How many fingers can I pour," I ask Celeste, "without setting a bad example for the kids?" She thinks I am joking, and she is not in the mood for joking. I am most decidedly not joking.

Soon the boys are sniffling and trooping up or down the stairs, as each either washes his hands but forgets to pee, or vice versa. Celeste warns us once again, in an increasingly strained tone, that the food is getting cold. Isaiah John is squawking again, despite being in my arms, because I won't give him the whisky bottle. He has realized that while I am often a big Daddy-barrel of fun, I am not equipped with lactating breasts. This being dinnertime and me being stingy with the whisky, he's decided he'd just as soon have Mama. I hand him off with an excuse about how I can't help it that he loves her more. She doesn't buy it.

Eventually we find our way to the table with clean hands, get water cups distributed, napkins placed, and the appropriate level of utensil technology before each child. We sit. There is talking and eating at the young heathen end of the table, until I remind them that we are going to bless the food, that we always bless the food, that we have been blessing the food since before they were born and have done so every day of their short lives, and that if they don't start remembering this soon their lives will not get any longer.

We hold hands. There is silence, for once. Isaiah John has been watching us pray these past weeks, and so now he reaches out his food-sticky hand and places it atop his mother's hand, which rests in my own. He smiles at me as he does it. I thank God for the food, though really I am thanking him for all of it — for the good and the bad and especially for them, without whom all my meals would be lonely and quiet and pointless. Then there is the sound of them eating and being fed, and I remember that in many churches Communion is referred to as "coming to the table." I wonder if this is how God feels when we come to his table, providing and being fed and being poured out all at once.

Caleb once won a gift certificate to a buffet restaurant. It was really just for one person's meal, but he was excited because he thought he had won a meal for the whole family. We didn't tell him otherwise; we just went to the buffet, and I made sure to pay without his knowing. Caleb smiled expansively at us as we sat in the restaurant, thinking he had fed the whole family. I know that feeling. It works something deep and healing into a parent's battered soul, the sound of his children eating while peace fills his house. It's a sin to take these times for granted. It's a sin to not seize every chance to sit with your family at a table covered with food and pray for God to sit with you there, and for your children — and you — to be fed with something more than just the simple food you see before you.

He ground flesh, *they say*
instead of color, *skin itself*
the luster he mixed

as grown men, transfixed
below the high transom
in The Calling of Saint Matthew

could only still their lives,
their faces straining toward his brush
which applied lucence like a poultice,

each stroke of color an unguent
to salve the pastiche of their human need
to the ochre of hallowed blessing.

It is that way with such rarity,
constraining each blush to a
rouge. I cannot move.

My skin takes on miracle
beneath your touch, sun
tincturing this room to wine.

I bear it—the burnished glaze
where your hand comminutes
want to umber, rubbing

each molecule till it hums itself
to a flame—a flicker on cheekbones,
shoulders, and balmed hip; votives

of table and wall and sill, where
the sun spills, its light ground down,
smoothing and riding each saddled edge.

Ruth Moritz, "Caravaggio Light"

3

Every Day a Baptism
the bathroom

It's generally true that a parent loves the sound of his children quietly playing and giggling. It means that they are happy, and occupied. This rule does not apply, however, to the bathroom. I tried, once, to explain to my children that it's called a *bath*room, not a *play*room. Caleb worked me over with that relentless deductive logic that he comes by honestly, noting that we let them play in their *bed*room even though it's not a playroom, and that most of the time we don't even take a bath in the bathroom, so why don't we call it a *tinkle*room or a *toothbrush*room instead, and isn't it better to play in the bathroom so that if you get dirty you can wash up right away, and why is it, Dad, that we have all these bath toys in here if we're not supposed to play? I soon reverted to *Because I said so*, which is an answer you don't really appreciate until you have children who are smarter than you.

If God is everywhere, then he is even — and perhaps especially — here, where we are daily humbled by our bodies, and by these quasi-autonomous and irrepressibly curious extensions of our bodies, our children. I suspect God is pleased to hear us resort to *Because I said so*, because he has been telling us the same thing from the beginning.

It's giggling that brings me to the bathroom now, where I find Caleb, the ringleader, standing at the toilet. Eli is to his left, and Isaac to his right. They are very excited about the fact that they are all peeing at once. They are pretending that their pee streams are light sabers. Their hips swivel back and forth as they engage in a pee-stream fight. "Look," Caleb announces with pride, "it's faster than taking turns." The sound of three streams hitting water becomes the sound of pee splattering its way across porcelain as each boy looks up at me, grinning. Here are all the stories of a bathroom captured in one moment, in this sight of three innocents peeing all over the floor their mother just mopped. These three boys, and you and I, along with everyone else, are beautiful and filthy at the same time. The bathroom is where this becomes easiest to see.

Respectable adults don't discuss what goes on in the bathroom. They understand that this is a matter of good breeding: only the ill-raised and untalented comedians talk about such things, after all, and we don't care to be associated with such rabble. Even the less polished among us are restrained by simple vanity: if you describe a bathroom activity, people can't help but imagine you doing it. Each of us would like the world to believe that he doesn't poo. At the very least, he would like for people to imagine him engaged in personal hygiene activities with elegance and grace, which likewise mitigates in favor of discretion.

But there is more to the bathroom than the worst parts of it, which is something that is also true about each of us. The bathroom, with all its attendant humiliations, is where we are cleansed as well as debased, and like so much else about our lives that is commonplace, it can sometimes be more than we are accustomed to thinking. Perhaps more than any other room in the house, the bathroom reflects the filth and chaos as well as the occasional beauty of who we are.

In our house the bathroom is often like a train station, what with the crowding right before any scheduled departure, and the officious pronouncements that go unheeded. (*All children out of the bathroom now!* Or, *The next person who uses my toothbrush is going to be in really serious trouble!*) And of course in any busy train station there are beggars, only instead they are my children, wheedling and angling for a doughnut because the cereal didn't take, and other parents let their kids eat doughnuts in the car, and honest, Dad, this time we won't get powdered sugar everywhere. Or perhaps they are agitating for a change in destination (instead of the grocery store, can we go to McDonald's?) or maybe for me to put shaving cream on their faces and help them shave using the blade-less razor I keep in my medicine cabinet for those rare times when I am feeling playful and we aren't already late for something. At the end of some days it feels as if I have spent more time with my children in the bathroom than in any other room of the house.

This is not by choice. Neither Celeste nor I have gone to the bathroom uninterrupted since 1998. It's almost as if there is a signal light over the door, announcing to everyone in the house under four feet tall that a parent is now available to chat. Children know that in this place you have no choice but to listen. I understand now why people call it a "throne" — I feel sometimes as if I am holding court. There are questions about who owns a particular toy, say, or whether finishing half a peanut butter and banana sandwich puts one in the running for dessert, or when—and I'm just asking, Daddy—it's okay to smack one's little brother. None of them seems to have any use for my dictates and pronouncements when I'm standing, but the moment my haunches hit the ring seat I'm transformed into Solomon of the Latrine.

A rookie parent locks the door, as I used to do. This only invites rattling, and knocking, and shouts of: *D-A-A-A-D-D-D-D! What are you doing in there?!?* For most males who survived adolescence, being questioned from the other side of the bathroom door evokes guilt regardless of what we are actually doing. The banging and shouting are not the worst of it, however, because eventually the banging stops, and I hear rustling, and then there are little fingers squeezed under the door, taking hold to rattle it in its frame. Then the challenge becomes not laughing, because once a child knows you think something is funny, he'll keep doing it.

The bathroom is where I am at my most absurd, and helpless, and ugly. Nobody wants people to see him like that. What's more, I know the rules of civility dictate that I chastise them for not respecting a person's privacy. (We are not animals, I sometimes growl at them, feeling very much like Quasimodo in my hunched-over, irritated state.) But often I laugh instead. I laugh at the ridiculousness of those grasping fingers wiggling beneath the door, powered by stubborn little wills. Our children still live in a world where mortification doesn't exist, and where it makes perfect sense to do whatever is necessary to get within touching distance of someone you love. They are like God in that way. I wonder, were we as unrestrained in our search for God, if we might not find him sometimes, right here with us, where he has been all along.

Unlike my wife and me in the bathroom, however, he seems pleased to be found.

My most frequent bathroom visitor has been Isaac. I think I have finally established some semblance of decorum, because now even he knows to keep his intrusions brief. He peeks his head in the door just to check on me. "Are you poopin', Dad?"

"Yes. Let me be."

"Okay." The door closes, but that's never the end of it. Sometimes he checks back on me thirty seconds later. "Still poopin', Dad?" Other times he lies on the floor outside the bathroom, sticks his feet on the door, and slides them in random patterns across its surface, creating a *swooshing* sound that reverberates between the walls around me. If he thinks I'm lonely he may toddle off to his room and return with a stuffed animal, which he props against the wall across from me before patting my knee and telling me to call him if I get scared. When I emerge, he asks me if I washed my hands, and when I answer yes, he whacks me affectionately on the leg and tells me, "Good job."

Perhaps they are so adamant about violating my privacy because I am most human here. We adults make it our life's work to elevate ourselves above the frailty and silly-heartedness of childhood, because that is what someone told us we are supposed to do. It's what we tell others to do as well; we admonish someone to *grow up*, after all, when we want him to be serious and responsible and less fun. But there is no room for pretense and self-importance when we are crapping or laughing or sleeping. Maybe this is why, when you get right down to the heart of it, children seek us out in those states of vulnerability. It is why they are so merciless about climbing into our beds when we are sound asleep, why they rattle the bathroom door when we lock it, why they do the same silly thing over and over once they've discovered it makes us laugh, as if our laughter is a treasure they have been seeking.

We yearn for a home infused with the sacred, but make the mistake of thinking sacredness is approached only by purging our humanity. We forget that we were created in the image of something sacred. We forget that God came to dwell among us, that we only ever find him in these rooms when we are like our children—vulnerable and vulgar and excreting, unencumbered by the notion that we are anything better than that. Instead of seeing God here, in the mess of ourselves, we scrub down and go looking for him somewhere else, as if we could ever get ourselves cleaned up enough to approach him were he the cold, distant, and demanding god we seem intent on making him.

The bathroom is where I've done a lot of cogitating on this topic, of course; it is the place where one is most likely to overthink things. It's also where a parent of small children finds himself explaining in gory detail what civilized people don't discuss. It's where you lead your child when he has an icky, which is what we call nose detritus in our house (*booger* being more low-brow than even we can tolerate). It's where you carry your child when he has an ouchie as well, so you can wash and bandage it and then pronounce on its seriousness to the inevitable crowd of curious siblings (*Is it still bleeding? Will he die? Did you ever have an ouchie this big, Daddy?*). The washing and bandaging usually aren't even necessary, but it's a tiny way of showing that you love them, and that you wish every wound lurking in their futures, waiting to hurl itself into their flesh, would land on your flesh instead. It would hurt less that way, wouldn't it?

The bathroom is our place of humiliation even when we aren't in it. I've had more than one serious, intellectual conversation with friends—the kind of conversation in which I used to shine, back before children and my job started turning me stupid—interrupted by a child bellowing from the bathroom: "D-A-A-A-D-D-D! Come wipe me!" There's no looking clever as you slouch off to wipe a three-year-old's butt. Nor in being summoned to inspect a five-year-old's wipe job. "Dad, does this look clean?" Caleb often asked during his transition to self-wiping. Cleanliness is next to godliness, I think to myself in these moments of degradation. And if God can see me in these moments, perhaps he will forgive all the times I supposed I was better than anyone else.

Despite their inherent grubbiness, my sons aspire, in their own way, to cleanliness. For a two-year-old this is simply a consequence of the novelty of hand washing. At one point we were going through a bottle of grape-scented children's hand foam every week, mostly due to Isaac. He was no cleaner for the effort. And don't even get me started on the fiasco that ensued when we endeavored to be good parents by investing in a bottle of bubble-gum-flavored children's mouthwash. Two days. That's how long it lasted.

As a result of all this we banned Isaac from unsupervised bathroom visits, to no avail. Sometimes I'd hear him in there regardless, water running at full blast, the smooth sound of its flow interrupted only by the frenetic wiggling of little fingers. His hand-washing philosophy follows that of shampoo manufacturers eager to sell more product: "Wash, Rinse, Repeat." He means well. This is what I remind myself whenever I approach the bathroom to inspect the latest disaster, at the center of which is, inevitably, Isaac. At least he's honest when he gets caught. Recently I came upon him, his belly pressed up against the counter, water soaking into his shirt and streaming off the countertop, toothpaste smeared over the mirror and in his hair, a toothbrush in each hand, neither of them his own. "Isaac," I bellowed, "what are you doing?"

"I don't know," he said with a sigh, surveying his mess. I know that feeling, don't you? We seem to have a purpose when we set out, but we get lost on the journey. I thought to myself, looking at my bewildered, toothpaste-sticky son: This is who I am to God. We trudge off to church in search of holiness, thinking that we've cleaned ourselves up and gotten our acts together, but this is what God sees—and he loves us, exasperating though we must be.

Though Isaac's brothers use less soap, they are just as convinced that one's hands only get clean when the water is on FULL BLAST. That common element aside, each has developed his own routine. Caleb rolls his sleeves up to his shoulders, more or less, because the little fussbudget can't abide wetness on his clothes. (Apparently they are made of the same material as the Wicked Witch of the West; I know this because he reenacts her woeful "I'm melting" routine whenever he spills anything on them.)

Caleb used to view hand washing as a good occasion to try out some new experimental monster faces, or maybe just have a discussion with himself. Once I peeked around the corner to see him making scarier and scarier monster faces, his hands curled into claws, dripping with soap. "Grrrrrr," he growled. Not satisfied, he leaned forward and adopted a fiercer scowl. "Grrrrrr!" He still wasn't happy. Leaning still closer, he intensified his glare, and summoned a deeper roar. "GRRRRRR!" He quickly shrank from the mirror, peeping: "Ooo, I scared myself."

Eli, meanwhile, is all business when it comes to hand washing. He needs coaching, however, or else he reverts to either the fingertips-only wash if he's in a hurry, or else the full-on surgeon's scrub-to-the-elbow routine if he's of a mind to be diligent. No matter which he chooses, it's always the case that the surface area he actually hits when rinsing will be approximately 50 percent of what he covered when scrubbing. Makes me itchy just thinking about it.

While each boy has a different hand-washing routine, they dry themselves in the same fashion, which is to perform this flippy-flappy motion with their hands, spraying the mirror and countertop with thick droplets. Then they get down from the step-stool, taking care to put their newly rinsed hands squarely in the puddle of soap they managed to drip on the edge. Finally, they hop, or run, or skip—but never simply walk—over to the towel and wave their hands around it while thinking dry thoughts.

I've never witnessed anything like it—these boys can worry a towel half to death, until it is wound up and wrinkled and just barely hanging from its rod, yet leave the bathroom with hands dripping wet. They're like those kung-fu masters who can hit somebody twenty times without leaving a bruise.

And that's what it feels like, roughly, to supervise hand

washing in our house. You anticipate many things about parenting—the sleeplessness, the worry, the dirty diapers. But you don't realize that getting several pairs of small hands clean will not only exhaust you, but make you seriously propose to your wife the theory that children two hundred years ago were much healthier for not washing their hands so often.

Though each of my sons is infested with perpetual dirt rings under the neck, cursed with stinky feet at a surprisingly early age, and besieged by a stickiness whose origin is always a mystery, they are drawn to water. This affinity gives me hope that one day they will all actually be clean at the same time, of their own volition. Parents have simple dreams like that—a house full of children who can wipe themselves effectively, for example, or who bathe without being asked, or who can make their own sandwiches.

Our children like water; it's just that we can't trust them with it. If we eliminated hand washing, there would still be toothbrushing, and squirt-gun reloading, and, in our house at least, science projects necessitating water. Even as I type this, Caleb has found me in the corner of our house where I hide to do my writing in the early morning hours. "I made a water clock," he tells me.

"What's a water clock?"

"Well, I took a plastic bottle, and cut a little hole in the bottom, and then filled it with water, so I can know what time it is by how much has drip-drip-dripped out."

"Oh." I survey him for a minute. He's so industrious. So diligent. So blissfully unaware of what his mother will do to both of us if she finds a homemade waterfall on his bookshelf. "You didn't put your new clock someplace where it will get water on things that shouldn't be wet, did you?"

Silence. A thoughtful countenance. This is soon replaced by a guilty countenance. He mumbles a few words about checking on something, and scurries away.

Caleb is just now learning to shower on his own, though his showers don't always take. I am the designated bather for this reason because, while Caleb can do relatively limited damage with a shower, you just don't want to let the smaller ones loose around a tubful of water. The job of bather, in our house, is a combination of lifeguard, referee, and bouncer. There is also some wrestling involved.

Our bathtime routine goes like this: While I rinse out the tub and run the water, the little ones busy themselves undressing, which frequently involves a Homer Simpsonesque "Doh!" when one of them whacks his forehead on the side of the tub while bending over to pull off his pants, or else panicked yelping when someone gets his shirt stuck halfway over his head. Sometimes when that happens I pull his shirt a bit further up, leaving the collar suspended around his hairline so that it looks like a colorful little nun's bonnet. The boys usually pretend that they have long hair when I do that and prance around buck-naked, except for those shirts dangling from the tops of their heads, talking in falsetto voices about their lovely hair. If they end up as cross-dressers, I know I'll have only myself to blame.

While his brothers are content with the standard assortment of plastic boats and various tiny sea creatures, Caleb as a toddler frequently insisted on bubbles — copious amounts of bubbles. He would watch me closely as I squeezed the purple plastic bottle of bubble juice into the tumbling stream of water, and at some point he would always tell me that it needed more.

"Just give it a minute," I would say.

"More. It needs *more*, Daddy. More bubbles."

"Fine. More bubbles."

Once the white foam had begun to mound and pile up in the tub, Caleb would murmur his approval: "B-u-u-u-u-b-l-e-s." This was usually followed by a hurried scramble to strip off underwear and socks. Thump. "Doh!"

When they are small I pick them up and lower them into the warm, swirling water, but as soon as he is able each boy likes to climb aboard himself. In the winter this is a delicate process, because the outside of that tub is cold. Only a three-foot-tall boy, you understand, can appreciate the full import of a cold tub. You know this by the way he stands on his tippiest toes, hands on the edge of the tub like he is mounting a dangerous steer, and gingerly — ever so gingerly — stretches over the frigid edge and into the warm water on the other side.

Then there is the washing, which is to say the splashing, with me barking at them to raise their heads so I can get the dirt under their chins, or to stop holding one another underwater, or to quit slinging water at me because I'm not the one taking the bath, as evidenced by the fact that *I have clothes on.*

Sometimes I am short-tempered with them because I am tired and they are not, and this doesn't seem fair. But other times I catch a glimpse of the sacredness in this act, this cleansing of my children. It's a parent's job, it seems, to keep as much of the muck of this world off our children as we can, for as long as we can. When a home becomes something more than living space, we begin to see the holiness of small acts — and God in the darkened corners. Sometimes, when I bathe them, I imagine I am washing away not just the dirt from our yard but the evils of a world that I think I can hear, when I listen closely, growling in anticipation. They are safe here with me, I think, and one day they will not be. The bathing, in those moments, becomes something more than a household duty. The tiredness isn't so bad, when I think about it like this, when I recognize that this blessing will pass away.

So while the bathroom is a humbling place, it can also be, at least sometimes, a sacred place.

Our bathroom, for example, is the place where we have washed each of our sons in sea salt, because this is what women used to do with their infants, carrying them into the Red Sea or the Mediterranean or the Atlantic and gently scrubbing them in the warm ocean water, its salt somehow cleansing them in a way that our modern soaps cannot. Perhaps this last is simply something we need to believe, that we have discovered a secret that will make their lives safer or easier or more complete, or simply more connected to the earth as it was intended to be, before generations of men were unleashed on it.

We did not wash Caroline with sea salt, because we didn't yet have any family traditions when she was born. Nor had we learned the fear of sickness and frailty and helplessness that is only imagination until you have lived it, after which it is a lingering wound, or shell-shock, or perhaps just a soul wariness every bit as tangible as the accompanying weariness. Much of our dabbling in healthfulness since her death — homeopathy

and reduced sugar and judicious denial of some inocula-
tions—was born of our new view of the world as a deceptively
treacherous place.

So we have washed each of our sons in sea salt, and perhaps it does nothing, but there is something sacred, nonetheless, in this ritual of washing. The bathroom is a place for
ritual as well as routine, after all, for sacredness as well as soap.
We last enacted this ritual with our infant, Isaiah John. It is
probably the final time we will do this; the doctors tell us that
more babies would be too hard on Celeste's health. Knowing
it was the last time lent the act a sweet sadness, which is probably true of everything that is approaching its end with your
child: the last nursing, the last days of reading to him, the last
time you hug him before he is married.

As we have done for each of Isaiah's brothers before him,
we scrubbed the interior of the bathtub until it shined, and
then we filled it with warm water. While I peeled off his layers
of clothing, Celeste poured crumbly gray sea salt into the tub,
so that the water seemed to take on a kind of weight, as well as
a lustrous, oyster-colored tint. Then she eased into the water,
and I gave her Isaiah. She cooed and soothed and held him
tight to quell the sensation of falling that haunts infants in the
beginning, so newly landed as they are in a fallen world. Then
we washed him, cupping the water with our hands and pouring it over his skin, gently rubbing his flesh—healing him
before he is ever sick. This is how we both think of it, though
we have never said so aloud. It's really more about healing
ourselves, I suppose, and the child we have lost.

I realized recently that I have probably prayed as much in the bathroom as anywhere else in the house. Most often it has been in the shower, as I prepare for a day, imagining how much misery work promises (*Please God, let me not kill anyone, or worse, tell them all what I really think of them*), or how draining a Saturday of yard work will be (*Precious Lord and Savior, let the wife be satisfied with the* first *place I plant each Hydrangea*), or how lovely it will be to go to lunch after church and then take a nap followed by all of us swimming, and me not at all uptight about the splashing (*Thank you, Lord; I know I don't deserve my wife, or these children, or this peace like a river*).

The shower was where I would cry and pray as our daughter lay dying, because its spray muffled the sound. My wife did the same. Each of us took our turn standing numb under the harsh flow of water and crying, the shower itself like tears. It's as if the world weeps with you, as if you are terribly alone and at the same time an object of empathy. Both of us took our turns standing and crying and praying, and sometimes cursing God, which is its own form of prayer, and a form that I like to believe he understands.

It is fitting that we come here to cry and pray, because the bathroom is where we are our ugliest and our most beautiful. It's where I urinate, and pick my nose, and squeeze zits. It's where my wife brushes her hair and puts on her lipstick, sometimes before she is fully dressed, looking luscious and lovely and bursting forth with every beautiful thing that a woman is. We have made love in the bathroom, and argued bitterly, and farted and primped and wept there. What better place to pray to our maker than in this room of mirrors and water, where we are simultaneously more and less than we let other people see, which is to say, our true selves? It's far better to come to God on the toilet, I think, in that state of profound humiliation, than puffed up and self-righteous in the front pew of our insular, lily-white, upper-class church. I like to think that God is less offended by the former than the latter. I need to believe that he sees all of these stories played out in our bathroom, and that he loves us in spite of, because of, what we are.

Thou, straggler into loving arms,
Young climber up of knees,
When I forget thy thousand ways,
Then life and all shall cease.

Charles Lamb, excerpted
from "Parental Recollections"

4

Where the Wild Things Are
children's rooms

I don't know why we assign these children separate bedrooms, because each seems to think that he belongs in *our*
bed. I know this because I am usually the person designated
to scoop up the wandering child and carry him back to his
rightful place after he clambers into our bed in the middle of
the night. I receive this authority from my wife, who is under
the impression that because she lugged them around inside
her flesh for nine miserable months, I can be imposed upon to
carry them a few yards back to their designated sleeping spots.
We all usually accept this without complaint — me because I
am not so idiotic as to argue with a sleepy wife, and the child
because all he really wanted in the first place was to be held. It
has occurred to me that I ought to discourage all this by making them march back through the darkness by themselves, but
no matter how sleepy I am, I haven't the hardheartedness to
do it.

After I lug one of our children back to his bed, I usually
kneel down beside him for a moment. I do this not because I
am exceptionally prayerful, but because I am bone-tired and
I just want to rest a spell. Tonight the culprit is Isaac, and so I

kneel down and press my face close to his, as if the sleepiness will seep through my skin and work its magic on this wakeful child. "Will you snuggle with me for a while?" he whispers. The offer is too good to refuse. His soft blond hair smells of baby shampoo, and it tickles my nose. He curls up in a ball and scoots into me until I almost completely envelop him.

The three of us fall asleep that way: Isaac, me, and my arm on which he has lain his head. It is the ache of my sleeping arm that wakes me again. I have to extract myself with just the one good arm, using it alternately to lift myself and drag my useless arm out from under Isaac's head. I have to be careful not to whack him upside the head with my dead arm, thereby waking him and repeating the entire cycle anew. Once I am safely out of his bed I tiptoe across the floor, taking care to avoid the places where it creaks like a haunted house. A little boy's floor in the middle of the night is like a minefield, what with the creaky spots, the murderous marbles, the treacherous Army men. I traverse it warily, holding out my one good arm for balance, and still I manage to embed a Lego between my toes. The trick in that moment is not to yelp.

It can be busy work, sleeping in our house. I suppose these children crawl into our bed because their parents are their safety. As we get older we come to associate comfort with our possessions, with our habits, with our own beds and our own stuff and the very familiar smells of our own surroundings. By the time we have reached our teenage years, if not sooner, we have come to see our own bedrooms as sanctuaries. But for these little ones, Celeste and I are still sanctuary.

That's probably for the best, because a wakeful child who tries to be self-sufficient at three in the morning can do more damage than one who just wants to snuggle. Isaac went through a period at two years old when he was up at least twice a night, sometimes more. Usually he would toddle into our bathroom, turn on the light, shut the door, and sit there on the floor. I have no idea why he did this. He had no idea. "Isaac, what are you doing?" I would mumble as I opened the door. He would stare up at me with a baleful look, Ducky clutched close to his chest. "I don't know," he would plead. Then he would hold out his arms and I would trundle him back to his bedroom, stumbling and groaning as I went. I would beg him not to get up again, to let his poor father have a rest. He would solemnly promise to comply. Then, once I reentered blessed REM sleep, he would get up again.

One night, perhaps out of pity, he decided to go it on his own. It was Celeste who found him in the kitchen. He was halfway inside the cupboard, rummaging through bags of crackers and boxes of cereal. "Isaac, what are you doing?"

"I don't know."

On the floor beside him were a spoon, a lollipop, and a cup of water. Celeste picked him up, turned off the kitchen light, and took him to the stairs. Halfway up the steps rested a small chair from the kid's table we keep in the kitchen. "Isaac, what's that chair doing there?"

"I don't know." This claim was becoming less believable.

Celeste made her way past the chair, Isaac in her arms, and noticed the kids' bathroom light was on. Their medicine cabinet open. "Isaac, what were you doing in the bathroom?"

"I needed some medicine," he declared. Piecing it together later, we surmised that Isaac wanted the cherry-flavored Tylenol for some imaginary ailment or another, only he couldn't reach it. So he went down to the kitchen to fetch a chair for use as a stepstool, but after wrestling it halfway up the steps he remembered that he would need a spoon for the medicine. Getting the spoon reminded him that he would be wanting a cup of water to wash down the medicine. The cup of water got him thinking about how nice a lollipop might taste in lieu of the spoonful of sugar that Mary Poppins advocates, but which Mom and Dad never administer at medicine time. Holding the lollipop reminded him that he was hungry for a more substantial snack. And so there Celeste found him, acting out his personalized version of *If You Give a Mouse a Cookie*.

So I suppose we should be thankful when they come straight to us in the middle of the night. I can't figure out what wakes them up, playing as hard as they do all day, and as blissfully free as they are of mortgage debt and work deadlines. If I had their arrangement I think I'd sleep like a baby. Come to think of it, why do we even use that term, sleep like a baby? I don't know about other people's babies, but mine aren't doing a whole lot of sleeping except when it's inconvenient to their parents, like when they nod off just as we pull into the Walmart parking lot.

Maybe it's the quiet, ironically, that sometimes gets to them. All day long they are immersed in one another's noises: yelling, wrestling, arguing, giggling, squealing, farting. I guess it can be unnerving to the brain, the deep silence of darkened mornings. I wouldn't know, of course, having long ago forgotten what deep silence sounds like.

There's the darkness as well that gets to them, as it does many children, as it did me as a child. At bedtime I have to do shadow checks, rearranging a jacket on a chair, or a ball lying next to the nightlight, because these objects cast eerie images on the walls and ceiling. I used to try the rationalist approach. (*See Eli, it's just a jacket. See how I'm moving it? Just a jacket. See?*) But children, or my children at least, are entirely comfortable with their irrationality. (*I know it's a jacket, Dad, but it's scaring me.*) So we do shadow checks, and occasionally I search under a bed or in a closet for monsters.

Eli likes to ask me what I'll do to a monster if I ever catch one in the house. He's tense when he asks it, because he believes if you say something terrible like "monster," you can actually make one appear, like it's just waiting beneath a rug or behind a coat rack for you to utter its magical, dreadful name. He relaxes as I recount the combination of gunfire, knife-fighting, and deadly kung-fu that I will unleash on anything that creeps into our home uninvited. Sometimes he embellishes my tale, adding that I can also chop the monster with a sword. I don't actually own a sword, but I haven't the heart to tell Eli.

Caleb used to be gripped by the same fear as Eli, that if you say the word "monster" one will appear. I would try to cure him of the fear by calling, "Hey monsters!" into a darkened closet or a shadowy room. Caleb would shiver with terror and excitement when I did this. The monsters never came out, of course, and so he and Eli would insist that I play the role of Tickle Monster. This involved my hiding in their darkened room and making growling, tickle-type noises while they worked up the nerve to come in and find me. In practice this meant that Caleb would exercise his elder brother author-ity, and so as not to risk decapitating the chain of command, he would send Eli in alone to do reconnaissance. Caleb will have a fine career in upper management.

In response to Caleb's order Eli would obediently creep into the room, giggling at my growls. Then I would pounce, he would squeal and try to run, and I would wrap him up in my arms. Caleb would squeal as well; I'm not sure why, since he was usually down the hall and out of danger. Upper-management material all the way.

Sometimes I would stay so well hidden that Caleb would come into the room to find out why it was taking Eli so long to get devoured, and then I would jump out and grab Caleb instead. Whenever I did this Eli would leap on my back in a desperate act of loyalty to his older brother. On occasion he had armed himself with a sword made of plastic or rubber or wood, making him a relatively dangerous little boy. He would whack me about the head and shoulders while I laughed and howled and secretly admired my son for his bravery in the face of so dreadful a Tickle Monster.

I think we dispelled the darkness that way, which is maybe how everyone does it, by inventing games and holding tight to one another. The older three boys go to sleep with relative ease now, but it used to be that when we tucked them in there was a sense that they imagined themselves going on a long, lonely trip. Maybe that's what sleep is for a little person. Maybe that's why they wrap their arms tight around our necks when we bend down to kiss them goodnight, because they don't know where sleep will take them. Maybe if we adults were less adept at entertaining ourselves with distractions, we would take bedtime this seriously too. Saint John of Damascus offered a bedtime prayer that many Christian Orthodox still pray. "O Master that lovest all men," he asked, "will not this couch be my grave? Or wilt thou again enlighten my condemned soul with the light of day?" It used to be that anyone who believed in a God of light would pray earnestly before bed. He would likewise pray with thanksgiving when he rose again from that bed that was not, for at least one more night, his grave. Now we seem to believe that bedtime prayers are just for children.

My sons have shown different ways of handling their nighttime fears. Isaac rubs the paw of his favorite stuffed animal along his face. When Eli was younger he would go to bed with a cowboy pistol in one hand and his blue blankey in the other. Sometimes for good measure he would also keep a sword under his pillow. As I shut his bedroom door I could hear him shooting at things in the darkness. *Click.* One dead monster. *Click.* Another down. More than once I woke to that sound in the middle of the night. *Click.*

I don't know what Eli saw, or where the nightmares of children originate. For we parents they come from what we have lived, and what has been lost, and what is still ours but might be taken. Sometimes I dream that one of my children has left his room in the middle of the night, walked out the front door, and disappeared into the darkness. I wake unable to breathe, and I can't get my heart to stop thundering until I have gone to each of their rooms and made sure they are still in their beds. Sometimes I gently put my quivering hand on a sleeping boy's head and pray. It's not an eloquent prayer, just a scared, half-witted plea to God that *he* keep the monsters of this world at bay.

I don't know for sure where the nightmares of children come from, but I suspect they come from us. Maybe our children sense our own fears, or maybe they see enough of our anger and grief that they learn to be afraid of us. When I was a boy, probably as a result of being dragged on too many occasions to hear some hell-obsessed Southern preacher, I began to have nightmares about demons. I would dream that I was playing in my room or walking along a hallway in my house, and suddenly everything would go dark—even if there had been sunshine outside; and there would be cruel laughter, and then the demons would come for me. For years I would go to sleep curled up in a tight ball, somehow having convinced myself that this was a method for keeping the demons away.

In my later years those dreams faded, but sometimes I still have them. I will think that I am awake as I lie in my bed, and a darkness will begin to creep into view. I know it's coming for me and I try to wake Celeste, to scream that there is something in our home; but no noise comes from my throat. I writhe in my sheets and try to scream. Finally my movement rouses Celeste, and she shakes me until I realize it's a dream, that there is no darkness beyond the absence of daylight. The darkness never gets to me before she wakes me up. I don't know what will happen the night that it does, but I know that as long as she's with me she will save me just in time. "I won't let the devil have you," she whispered to me once, back when I thought she was going to leave for good. This is one reason I selfishly hope to die before her. I don't think I would do well in a world without Celeste.

I used to think the nightmares were unique to me, until one day my father—he had reappeared, and we were cautiously trying to learn how to be something like blood relatives—told me that he used to have similar dreams. I had revealed a dream so terrifying that I'd spent half the day thinking I was crazy, that any moment I might begin screaming and never stop. He told me about a dream that left him so certain dark things were coming that he made my mother drive him to the middle of an open field, just to be away from every shadow. I guess all of us would prefer to be away from shadows, though we can never be free from our own.

And maybe we can never be entirely free from the shadows of our parents, either. Lately Caleb has been coming to my room in the darkest part of morning. He wants me to pray for him because he is having nightmares.

This makes me want to weep. I thought that, if nothing else, I could protect my children from the world I knew growing up. When Caleb comes to me with that haunted look, I can't help but think that my sins are finding their way onto his shoulders. I feel like I have failed to root something dark out of myself, and in that failure I have passed it down to my son. I recall a warning in the Bible that the sins of the fathers shall be visited upon the children.

When Caleb comes to me like this, I take him back to his room and we kneel down beside his bed. I put my hand on his troubled head and I call on the Holy Spirit of God to protect my son, my children. I pray for peace to wash over him. I pray that he will know he is forever in the arms of his loving Father. I pray these things so that Caleb will hear them. I also pray, in the quiet, broken places of my heart: *Forgive me for the things I have done. Have mercy on this child. Lord, have mercy.*

Then God gives a temporary mercy at least, because praying like this seems to put Caleb's heart at ease. He crawls into his bed and smiles contentedly. He doesn't ask, but I get him a stuffed animal. I kiss his face and tell him I love him. He loves me back. Are you ever amazed at how effortlessly they love us back, given how often we fail them, how often we bark at them, how often we make them less important than they ought to be? What would the world look like if all of us were so forgiving?

What would we parents give to keep these children from the darkness? Many of us would fly straight down into hell if we thought it would save them. I'm sure a great many pastors disapprove of that sentiment, but these dark morning hours are when we are most apt to whisper the truth to ourselves, and there is my truth. I would go to hell for my children. And this is how we know the love of God, that he did the same for his little ones, faithless though we are.

When the daylight pours through our windows it is easy enough to put aside the thoughts of fear and darkness. As I write this, the horizon is beginning to come alive with blues and purples, backlit by the faintest orange. I am in my office, preparing to put aside writing for another day of work, and at home my children are beginning to stir in their beds. Soon Caleb will wake first, and he will play with robots or lounge in bed reading *Hank the Cowdog*, until he remembers we have an actual dog that he is responsible for feeding in the mornings. Caleb has no ability, it seems, to be quiet, and so soon Eli will be awake as well. He will lie in his bed and perhaps stretch his soft blue blankey over his face as a way of blocking out the light, just as he uses it at night to ward off the darkness.

In their bedroom, meanwhile, Isaac and Isaiah will eventually wake one another up as well. Isaiah will wake first and hoot from his youth bed until Isaac comes over to play with him, or Isaac will get up and start rummaging around, either for clothes or for a piece of gum that he managed to sneak past us the night before. One morning I caught him strolling out of his bedroom, eating a biscuit. "Where'd you get that biscuit?" I asked.

"I accidentally took it to my room last night," he said, as if that's what regular people do. Sometimes it's food, but usually it's chewing gum, which is his most favorite food item. We have to do a mouth check before bedtime, because Isaac sees nothing abnormal about going to bed with gum in his mouth.

If he's not scrounging for food then he's donning what is likely only the first of many changes of clothes. In every other way this boy is a Viking, but in couture he is like a fashion model. It is his own personal sense of fashion, mind you, but it is fashion nonetheless. One morning he may emerge wearing two T-shirts beneath a sweatshirt, and you will have to send him back to his room because it is the middle of July. Or he will come out sporting silky basketball shorts and a tank top, only to be told that it is Sunday, that it is the dead of winter, and that shooting hoops is not allowed in church.

His predictable response is to go completely slump-shouldered and stomp back to his room, as if his parents are responsible for the weather or the day of the week. Unless it's sleeping time, Isaac doesn't care to stay in his room. He views being sent there for any reason as punishment. He far prefers to be in Caleb and Eli's room, which is where all the action is. If he can slip past his mother in whatever getup he's chosen for the morning's attire (by lunchtime he will have changed into something entirely different if he can get away with it), he will head straight for his brothers' room.

Sometimes when I come home from work they are all crowded in there, even baby Isaiah John. They are occupied with building something or listening to music or maybe each of them is engaged in a quiet enterprise that has more meaning because it is in the company of his brothers. I stand outside the doorway and listen as Caleb reads to the littlest ones, or Eli explains that they are all going to be pirates now with the beds as their ships. Sometimes there is just the gentle sound of pages turning, a baby cooing, Legos being clicked into place.

Because they are boys and they are sinners, of course, there are often times when what I hear is carping and complaining. "That's my book, Eli," Caleb gripes.

"You said I could borrow it," Eli fires back.

"Let's play spaceship," Isaac whines.

"Get out of our room," his brothers reply, this being the only thing on which they agree.

"You're not the boss of me," Isaac retorts. "*God* is."

It's still more civil than the U.S. Congress or the United Nations, but a parent listening to this can't help but feel like a failure. So I go in and gripe at all of them about how they ought to be pleasant and stop griping.

They are too young to appreciate the irony. I am too irritated and tired to realize it until later, when they are all asleep. Some of you know what it's like to lie in your bed waiting for sleep, picking over all the places you screwed up as a parent that day. That's when it hits me in a big wave of shame, the fact that my children are likely responding to one another the way they see Celeste and I treat each other, the way we treat them.

Children are a painful barometer in that regard, aren't

they? Likely as not when they are behaving like grumpy little trolls, it's because we parents have been full-grown trolls ourselves. I remember how in those ugly days, when Celeste and I were fighting our way toward divorce, Caleb turned angry and violent. He would refuse instruction, and pull away if you put a hand on him. Eli went the opposite direction, receding into himself, becoming silent and mournful. I didn't notice it at the time because I was so enveloped in my personal melodrama, but my children were living out my emotions. I had brought anguish into our home and it was living with us. In many churches the adults have a habit of asking one another how they're doing, but it seems to me that if you want a truthful answer you should look at the children.

Right now they are at peace, which is a reflection, I hope, of peace between Celeste and me. Peace has been present a lot lately, though sometimes the past will come roaring back at us like something vicious that rushes at you in the darkness, and we will have to resist the impulse to give ourselves over to it. For now, though, we have peace as the day is settling down for rest. We have finished dinner, the evening chores and music practices are done, the baths have been administered, the entreaties that they please, for the love of God, put on pajamas and brush their teeth, have been mercifully heeded at last, and the stories have been read to the littler ones.

Eli and Caleb are upstairs conspiring in their traditional stalling routine. I think they do this subconsciously; to think otherwise is to imagine them capable of extreme cruelty. Their stalling might take the form of telling me long stories about what they've read or what happened while I was at work, even though we had the entire dinnertime for those tales to be recounted. Alternately they might ask me what, for little boys, are real posers, like why the clouds hang motionless sometimes, or why the garbage men come only once a week, or why the preacher gets to stand up and talk every Sunday instead of other people getting turns. When they tell their stories or ask their questions, they come to a complete halt in the getting-ready-for-bed process, which is how I know they are stalling. So I will answer them abruptly and hurry them along so that Celeste and I will have fifteen blessed minutes of quiet before one or both of us falls asleep.

Sometimes the delay takes the form of a lost blankey or Lamby or some other cherished item. We learned long ago not to tell the pining child to go without, as this sets him to wailing and invites remonstrations from his brothers about what cruel parents we are. When one of these love objects goes missing we form a search party, and usually we find it under a pillow, or in the playroom, or occasionally in the minivan.

One night, however, Isaac's beloved Ducky disappeared for good. It was his favorite companion, this little stuffed duck. You could tell when he was sleepy or simply wistful by the presence of that duck in his hands. He would hold it close to his face, like it possesses a residual mother-scent, or perhaps so it could smell him and be reassured. Isaac would kiss his duck, and pet his duck, and for some inexplicable reason he would whack his duck against his chin. When the sentiment came over him he would love on that duck the way a new mother dotes on her infant, except, of course, for the whacking part. Isaac loved Ducky.

Then he lost the lousy quacker. Our search began earnestly enough, but to no avail. We escalated it as he began to wail. We recruited his older brothers to the rescue effort. Maybe he put it in a pot under the stove, we thought. Perhaps it got dropped in someone's shoe in the closet? No luck. Our search grew to encompass the trash. I got a flashlight and searched the front yard, the sides of the house, the backyard. No Ducky.

Isaac's love for his duck was nothing compared to a parent's love for his child, but he didn't know that, and so when I told him Ducky couldn't be found, he wept like someone had stolen his baby. We wanted to shed tears too, listening to him cry himself to sleep that night, as well as the next. We tried desperately to get him to attach his affections to some other stuffed animal. How about this other duck? Winnie the Pooh? Mickey Mouse? Eventually he gave grudging attention to his lamb, who in due course was christened Lamby. They got along fine enough, and over time the pain of the lost duck abated—so long as nobody mentioned him.

Months later, we found Ducky. He had fallen behind a bookcase. We celebrated the return of our prodigal duck. I think at some point Celeste and I had come to miss him more than Isaac did, because our celebration was more exuberant. Isaac had moved on to a new love, but he gave Ducky a hug all the same, and introduced him to his new best friend, Lamby.

Celeste was bound never to endure this heartache again. She confiscated Ducky until she could sew a little blanket to his back, the goal being to make him harder to misplace. Now Ducky looks like he's wearing a giant cape. He's not just an ordinary Ducky anymore. He's Superducky.

Sometimes I walk through their bedrooms when they are gone somewhere, or when they are playing outside. I look at their treasures, their bottle caps and rubber bands, robots and model cars, rocks and blocks and odd-looking packaging materials that they secreted into their pockets before their mother could throw it all in the trash. I ponder the books they are reading and imagine the adventures in their minds, and it all feels like a second chance, which I suppose it is, in more ways than one.

We don't have a room for Caroline anymore. We left that house years ago, and when we came to our new house it didn't seem right to set up her things in a room that had never known her. It seemed right to let go in that way. Sometimes I wish I could return to her room, which I suppose is a faint shadow of the yearning to hold her again. I used to go into her room after we lost her, put my face into the shirts and dresses hanging in her closet, and breathe in her smell. I would lie on her bed and put my face on her cool pillow. You don't realize how much you miss someone's scent until happenstance carries a likeness of it to you, and then you are crying and it takes you a moment to realize why.

Her things are shadows of her. When I brush her empty dress with my palm, I am touching what once touched her tender skin. When I open her dresser drawer and pick up a hair barrette, my hand forms itself to the curls of hair that disappeared before she died. If I put my hand inside her shoe I can feel the imprint left by her toes. These things whisper, *She was only just here*, and also, *She is gone*.

I used to sit in her room, after she was gone, and close my eyes. I imagined that she was playing downstairs, that any moment she would come bounding up the stairs and leap into my arms. I looked at her doll in the rocking chair, the pictures of her friends on the wall, and thought to myself that this is where she belongs, that sooner or later she would have to come back, if I only waited still and quiet and hopeful. I sat on her bed where we prayed at night, and I wondered whether she might have lived if only I had prayed harder, or been less sinful, or taken her less for granted. I imagined her in heaven and wondered if she missed me there.

P.F. Thomése observes in *Shadowchild* that we call "orphans" those children who have lost parents, and we call "widow" or "widower" that person who has lost a spouse, but we have no name for the parent who has lost his child. Perhaps this is because it is the only way we know to signify its unspeakable nature, by leaving it nameless. Our children come to us from their rooms when they are lonely and afraid in the night, but where can we go when they are gone? There is only where they have been, and it is filled with echoes and shadows. All our tears can give it no more life than that.

I miss Caroline's room, but it is probably best that I can't go to it anymore. Surrounded by those dead shadows, it might have been harder for me to hear her voice in Isaac's belly-laugh, or feel her dancing in Isaiah John's wiggle, or see in Eli and Caleb what she might have looked like when lost in a book, or intently chopping tomatoes, or playing the piano with purposeful fingers. We can get lost in the dead shadows of things and lose sight of the living memories around us. Life sometimes gives us new memories, not by way of replacement, but perhaps to ease our remembrance and to remind us that joy has always been married to suffering—since the day the

Devil first tried to devour the world. I see Caroline in each of her brothers, and sometimes I hug them a little tighter for it. They like being loved, and so they don't ask why. I hope they'll never need to understand it.

This room has grown deeper, has grown larger.
In the presence of awe it has become somewhere more holy.
It has become somewhere where rest is possible.
Through my hands and through my breath the walls have
    moved back,
the ceiling has lifted. The doorway has located itself.
Now there is no need for anyone to wander lost, here.
Everywhere I look I see wonder. The window is shuttered
but the room, the landscape is bright enough for any activity.
I ask only one question here — here amongst all this peace
and amongst all this time and space and light and love,
how will it ever be possible for me to sleep?

A.F. Harrold, "Room Poem, #1a"

5

Rest for the Weary

our bedroom

It is early morning, and nearly everyone is asleep. I have curled myself around Celeste, and I am gently kissing her shoulder. "I'm still sleeping," she growls. It is part informational, part warning. I content myself to massage her back, in that vague, unrealistic hope men have that a half-hearted back rub can turn women into passion-drunk vixens. It enters my mind that the definition of insanity is to do the same thing over and over, hoping for a different result. Celeste growls again.

Someone knocks at the door. It's Eli. He is clutching his blue blanket and sucking on his two middle fingers, which is what he does when he's sleepy or scared or sad. Eli is my melancholy child. He wants to snuggle.

I believe children have a deep intuition that sounds an alarm whenever their mother and father feel amorous. This is accompanied by a genetic impulse to disrupt these liaisons, lest they face even more competition for our attention. When most people hear about those peculiar families with fifteen or twenty children, they blame the parents for having more children than they can possible manage. I blame it on defective children. My wife and I can't even hug without at least one child wedging himself between us. "Close me!" This is what Caroline used to say, wiggling between our bodies when she caught us in an embrace, basking in the feel of being bound up tight in love.

Each new child doesn't just add to the likelihood that someone will be awake in the middle of any given night or at the crack of dawn; it multiplies the odds. And the thing about wakeful children is that they very much need for you to share that experience with them. So how did these parents who ended up with twenty kids find the time or energy to make the last dozen? I think scientists will eventually discover that the children in those families are missing whatever genetic component compels Eli to wake, on this particular morning when I'm thinking my backrub mojo may actually work, and decide he wants to snuggle. It's the instinct that leads my sons to wrestle one another out of that prime position between Mom and Dad on the couch, or sidle up next to me in order to whisper in a conspiratorial voice: *Daddy, we should leave the others here with Mom and just you and me go somewhere.*

What I'm suggesting is that nature has given us an outstanding form of birth control: children. Having three or four kids may not completely sap your desire to have more, but it certainly reduces the opportunities, if only because each child seems set on limiting his competition. What happens in our bedroom, therefore, is of great interest to them.

A friend who counsels couples once told me that when men go to the bedroom, it's for one of two things, neither of which is talking. For a woman, on the other hand, the bedroom is a sanctuary. It's a place to unburden her soul. A husband's ears, I have learned, are essential to that unburdening. Add children to the mix and suddenly there are wildly disparate demands being placed on a single room, making it alternately a sleeping lounge, tawdry motel, therapy center, and — especially if Isaac has gotten into my Cocoa Puffs before invading our privacy in the morning — the chimpanzee exhibit. All of this makes our bedroom the San Andreas Fault of our marriage.

W e didn't expect the bedroom to bear so much stress before our kids came along. When we were still childless, Celeste and I could nap in any room of our house. We could also make love in any room, whenever we felt like it. We didn't necessarily live out that freedom, mind you, but it was nice to have those rights on paper.

There was also plenty of space to talk. If Celeste needed to get something off her chest about work, or her relatives, or — only rarely, of course — something I might have said or done, we had all the time in the world, and no audience of midgets following us from room to room, soaking it all up so they could leak it later by asking Grandma, perhaps, how she got *co-dependent* and if she needs to get a shot for it, or reporting to their uncle that even though Mom and Dad aren't going to loan him any more money, he can always have some from their piggy banks.

Once children are pitter-pattering through the house, those freewheeling discussions and arguments and rare, but sweet, horseplay on the couch all go by the wayside. They get crammed into the bedroom, with the added complication that your children can hear the click of your door latch even when they are sleeping at a friend's house across town. Private conversation, and arguments, and other intimate activities that are just as much the cement to a relationship as communication—all of these things get compressed in space and time once you become a parent.

I confess that I am the primary reason the kids view our bedroom as an indoor playground. Sometimes I seize them up like I am a ferocious wrestler, and growl as I lift them over my head, spinning around while they squeal. Then I hold them close to my chest and pretend to body slam them on the bed, though in reality I am just placing them on their backs and then tickling and kissing them all at once. "Do it again!" The happy victim shouts, which always brings the others running, so that I become like a ride at the state fair. I'll give each boy in turn his requisite body slams until someone gets the cunning idea to jump on my back while I am bent over tickling his brother, at which point I become like the monkey bars, until I collapse and the whole thing turns into a wrestling/tickling free-for-all on the bed and surrounding area, with Mom's pillows serving the function that folding chairs serve in major wrestling events.

There was also the time, not long after giving the older ones cowboy guns and toy rifles, that I showed them how to convert our bedroom into a fort. We stretched the bedspread from the bed to a chair and anchored each end with pillows to give us a roof. Then we stacked more pillows at the entrances.

"Count your ammo, boys," I told them. They weren't sure what I meant, but they tried to look serious and soldier-like. Soon we were capping bad guys, the boys working the short-range fire and me on the sniper rifle. Occasionally one of us would get shot, but never mortally. Our rule is that you don't die if someone patches you up quick. Getting patched up means getting tickled in whatever location you've been shot. Wouldn't it be nice if it worked that way in real life?

Eventually their mother came in, drawn by the shouts and the spitting sound little boys make when they are trying to do shooting noises. We had wrecked the bedroom. It's probably more accurate to say that we had wrecked *her* bedroom. Fortunately, though Celeste is a neat freak, there's something in her that is deeply moved by the sight of men defending their castle. Had I been playing fort by myself, of course, the outcome might have been different, but in this case she kissed each of us on the forehead, and then went to fetch the camera. It made me wonder if back rubs have been the wrong strategy all along. Do they make cowboy gun belts in my size?

Children don't always come to play or to get your attention, of course; sometimes they just want to observe as you dress or make the bed. I don't know why it eludes so many of us that children simply crave our nearness. I used to think that every moment with my children should be one in which I am doing something entertaining or educational, but I realize now that sometimes they just need to draw close, as if I am a safely rooted old tree or a crackling fire on a cold night. Celeste and I like to believe that we are giving them a world that was alien to us. Neither of us has memories of being held in the loving arms of both parents at once, but this is a commonplace for our own children. We often pray, *Let it end with us.* I suppose we are also asking of God, *Let it begin with us.*

The problem with all these observant children underfoot

is that anything ridiculous I do is now recorded in the minds of one or more children. And children are like paparazzi, because they will share your business with the public. A story still making the rounds thanks to Caleb and Eli concerns my encounter with a spider. For the record, that spider was a brown recluse, which can give you a very nasty bite. I saw him on my shirt as I pulled it from my closet one morning. The two aforementioned witnesses were sitting on my bed. When I saw the spider I cautioned them in a manly voice, and then shook the shirt to make the spider fall onto the floor, where I aimed to squish him like the bug that he was.

I shook my shirt, and the spider was gone. I looked all about me, the boys serving as spotters from the safety of the bed. He had vanished. "Must have gotten back into the closet," I speculated. The boys concurred, disappointed there was to be no spider-squashing. I double-checked the shirt, then slipped my arms in. It was only as I began to button it that I spied the spider. On my T-shirt. Crawling toward my face.

At this point, given the rumors that have come out of that fateful morning, I want to point out that many warrior traditions involve a high-pitched screech of fury, evoked to strike fear in the heart of the enemy. To the untrained child's ear, such a warrior yell might indeed sound as if Dad "squealed like a girl," which is how Caleb tells it. He likes to reenact what he thought was a panicked flurry of slaps at my own chest, but which in reality was a series of well-timed judo chops. Eli in turn mimics Caleb mimicking me, and then they both squeal like girls and fall out giggling. My sons have no sense of discretion.

These childish invasions are not always bad. If Celeste and

I are in that peaceful awake-but-not-up state, then nothing is sweeter than to hear a whispered conference on the other side of our door — the boys discussing whether we are awake and if it's okay to go in, the oldest urging the youngest to sneak in, reconnoiter, and report back. This is always followed in short order by the lot of them trooping in, a merry little procession, their hearts full of cheerfulness because they haven't yet learned the adult habit of resenting daybreak. They are chirpy and gentle, and if we were diligent parents the night before, then they smell of soap from last night's bath — an aroma frequently overlaid, in Isaac's case, with the smell of whatever he has cribbed from the pantry to stave off his first-thing-out-of-bed hungries. They clamber onto our bed and find their places on top of or between or beside us, and there is hugging and kissing, as if sleep had carried us all far away from each other, and this is our reunion.

Whenever we sing "Come Thou Fount of Every Blessing" in church, this is what my mind goes to — these moments when we are all in the big bed, the children rolling over one another and us like logs, or perhaps hopping about and tackling each other while I try to protect my sensitive parts from their feet, which are small, but strike like little ball-peen hammers. *Here* is my every blessing, I think as the hymn is sung, and then always give my whispered prayer: *Thank you.*

Sometimes there is no commotion, just the bunch of us lying in bed with our arms and legs over and under and between each other like pickup sticks. The children ask us questions about whether they'll go swimming today, or if our mothers and fathers ever made us pancakes for breakfast, or, Daddy, did you just walk up and kiss Mommy the first time you saw her? In reply we often find that we are telling them the stories of our lives, which is much of any parent's conversation with his child, the truths and wishes and mistakes that he has endured or seen. We tell them our stories with a hope that somehow the thousand futile things we have done or endured were really a preparing of the way, so that they might have an easier time of living when they leave us.

The children want to be face-to-face with us when they are in our bed. Sometimes one of them will lie beside me, which is always sweet but precarious, because the legs of little boys seem to be autonomous. As we lie there he will put his hands on my face to feel the stubble, or perhaps the vibration in my jaws when I speak, and he will watch me with those deep chocolate-brown eyes each of our children has, and it will occur to me that I am experiencing what may be the best part of the day, or of our lives, together.

I try to listen carefully to what they have to say in these moments, and to etch their voices into my memory. Even if most of what they say is about trivial matters like toys or cartoons or whatever naughty thing the neighbor boy did and got away with, they always relate it with such gravity, and it seems to me that we parents make a mistake when we discount the opinions of a child. "Many holy things lie in ruins," writes Frederick Buechner, "because the world has ruined them and we have ruined them." Surely this includes one of the holiest things of all, the relationship between a parent and child. So I try my best to listen. Eli recently told me, during one of those quiet snuggle times: "I'm not afraid of monsters, or of a witch."

"That's good," I tell him. "They should be afraid of you."

"Yeah, cause I have my sword and my gun."

"Yep. You are one tough little cowboy-knight."

"No, I'm a knight-cowboy."

"Right."

"And if they get me you will come save me."

"Yes, I will. But they won't get you."

"Okay." He sucks his fingers while we watch each other. His fingers come out with a gentle *pop*. "Can we have blueberry muffins for breakfast?"

Are our adult problems and hopes really that much more consequential to God? And yet he listens, I think, and knowing this can often be more important than the answer itself, should it ever arrive; an answer to our fleeting complaint about a fleeting life. This is why I try to listen with a seriousness that matches their own, even if the topic is the unfairness in Dad eating Cocoa Puffs Saturday mornings while everybody else gets whole-grain Cheerios. I suppose I will never have the wisdom of the first father I admired, Michael Landon's character in *Little House on the Prairie*. I used to wish that Pa Ingalls was my father, and as I grew older I imagined that one day I would be a father like him. Only when I was older still, did I learn that Michael Landon wasn't Pa Ingalls either.

When Isaac was a newly walking baby, he went rooting through my closet one day, and he came clomping out in a pair of my shoes. His chubby little feet disappeared inside them. As he struggled to walk and keep his balance, it occurred to me that this is every father, and perhaps every mother, just trying to get by in shoes we can never hope to fill. "Trust me, little man," I told him, "they never get any smaller."

The shoes will always be too big, and I'll probably never

be very wise, but at least my children will remember, I hope, that I listened to them. Maybe that will be enough. Maybe when they are older they will still bring me their problems and griefs and joys, and though I will be no more able then to make their worlds safe and complete, I will still get to listen. This is a privilege I think we parents often forget is ours until it is lost. Our children have their own stories to tell, you know.

Each child is different in these moments, though all seek out this closeness. With Caleb one is struck by the sense that his mind never really turned off during the night. He has a lot of ground to cover when he awakens and tracks me down. He tells me about things he wants to build, and the supplies he needs — *today, as soon as breakfast is done, Dad* — to build his inventions, and how it makes good sense for us also to go fishing and play chess and assemble a model airplane as well, and then, after lunch, we can build a catapult and see if it will launch the cat into that big tree beside the driveway. Caleb makes lots of hand motions when he describes his plans, even when he is lying beside me in the bed. His eyes get big at the really important or momentous parts of his monologue, and all the while he is watching me, to be sure that I am really listening, really hearing him. Maybe they are always watching that closely, and I only notice when I have no distractions, just this little boy lying beside me, opening up his still mostly unwounded heart, so that even a self-centered introvert like his father can see that now is the time to listen, truly listen, even though everyone in the family knows I have a hard time doing that for very long.

Though sometimes he wants to talk about monsters and blueberry muffins, Eli is usually content to lie beside me and stare. He clutches his blue blanket and sucks his fingers and watches me, his nostrils blowing gentle puffs onto my skin. He speaks less frequently than the others, but I don't think he has fewer total words to share, because sometimes the words pour out of him like a burst dam. This always reminds me that he is forever pondering, that he is my thoughtful worrier, looking the least like me in body but being most like me in spirit.

Isaac, meanwhile, can only be motionless for a few seconds at a time. There's wrestling to be done, after all, and God gave him that chunky body and low center of gravity for a reason. He scrunches up beside me like his brothers, but this is usually so he can whack me on the back or the arm or on top of my head, which is how he shows that he loves you and has missed you, by whacking you or by squeezing you as hard as his muscles will allow. Once Isaac has found his way into our bedroom, we don't get much peace. He climbs onto the bed and begins jumping, whether or not it has been made and adorned just so with the numerous pillows my wife believes are essential to good housekeeping. Isaac jumps whether or not we are stretched out on it comfortably, and heedless of his personal safety, as well as the safety of anyone else who might be within landing, tackling, whacking, or hugging range. Isaac has plenty of words, but I think he communicates mostly through physicality. I don't know how two introverts could have produced such a hugger, but then I never really did understand genetics. Perhaps we have an inveterate people-person somewhere in our lineage. Probably on my wife's side.

Baby Isaiah John is, like his brother Isaac, a tumbler. He

has to be lifted or hauled onto our bed where he immediately begins toddling about, skating close to the edges so that Celeste or I or both of us are constantly correcting his course and retrieving him in the nick of time, which is just the way he likes it. When he is not making us rescue him he is likely sitting on my head and pulling my ear. This is until he remembers that God made bananas, and begins asserting his right, in no uncertain terms, to a banana for breakfast, which amounts to saying "Nana, nana, nana?" over and over in a rising pitch until someone relents and gets the little monkey what he wants. He hasn't yet learned to appreciate the still quiet, this one. We are all of us looking forward to the day when he does. Even the chaos that intrudes once he's found his way to our bedroom, however, is its own kind of peace.

I read somewhere that most parents who bury a young child see their marriages dissolve. This makes no sense. You'd think we would cling all the tighter to one another. But grief and anger are like the cancer that stole our child, twisting you into something you weren't meant to become. It was fitting, I suppose, that our bedroom is where things began to come undone, because it was in our bedroom, on our bed, that we watched our daughter die.

I remember lying beside Caroline late one night, one of the last nights we had her, back when I couldn't imagine one day having a bed full of rambunctious boys. The tumor had taken her ability to move or speak. I was overwhelmed by the sense that I had failed her. "Have I been a good Daddy to you?" I asked her this, knowing she couldn't reply. I searched her eyes for something that could serve as an answer. Something you don't expect is how guilty you feel when your child is dying. Reason doesn't matter in this equation; your flesh knows that it is supposed to protect your child, and your heart dies as she dies. This is how it feels.

We prayed over Caroline in our bed for weeks, surrounded by medications and medical equipment, asking God for a miracle. We even anointed her with oil. Everything the Bible instructs you to do when someone you love is deathly ill, we did. Still her cancer brought us mercilessly to that final moment when Caroline lay in her mother's arms on that bed, her eyes fluttering as if she was trying to open them, the last breaths wheezing in and out like ragged sighs, and me giving her permission to die.

Then she was gone. What remained with us on that bed was only the limp body of a three-year-old girl, swollen and twisted by cancer into something little girls should never become.

It's not something you can easily ask a preacher: *How do I forgive God?* It's not an allowable emotion for most of them, that we could be angry at God. Anger is a normal enough reaction, but there's something wrong with directing it toward God, and so many preachers seem to want to inoculate us by pretending that funerals are really big celebrations, if only we'd look at them correctly. I recently went to the funeral for a twenty-three-year-old woman, killed by cancer. The preacher wanted us to smile. She is in heaven now. Things are wonderful for her. Our lives here aren't permanent anyway. Rejoice. I wanted to punch him.

I believe all the things he said are true, but we aren't

designed to bury our children. We weren't fashioned to rejoice when we put them in the dirt. All the head knowledge of a theologian departs when you are cleaning the corpse of your child, which is what we did in our bedroom on the night she died. We cleaned her and dressed her and then in a fury I gathered all the medical equipment that had come to decamp in our home and I shoved it into a closet. I carried her downstairs to our friends who had rushed over from all parts of town upon hearing the news, and they wept as they watched me put her on the undertaker's gurney. He wheeled her out the door and when we saw her again she was a hollowed-out wax figure, cool and hardened to the touch, like a candle that has been blown out and laid in the drawer.

How do I forgive God? This is the question you ask yourself in the dark hours as you lie in your bed, the adrenaline which had afforded you energy to bury your dead and dutifully nod when the preacher told you to *count it all joy* now drained away. You are angry. If you believe in a God who can work miracles then you are angry at him, because he didn't give you a miracle. You are angry at God but you desperately need to be right with God, if only because you believe — or maybe just a slender part of you still believes — that there is a heaven, and that this is where the person you long for is waiting. So you ask the heretical question of how you forgive God, but likely as not you ask it only to yourself, because most people who hear it feel their Christian duty is to correct you.

I couldn't answer this question for the longest time. I felt like a beaten child, and it filled me up with anger. This anger became a hateful wedge between Celeste and me. It became a storm filling our house, and its epicenter was our bedroom.

This is probably always the case in every family near its end. The bedroom is where most of us create a family, and very often it is the place where we begin to undo that family.

In this way the stories of our bedroom become the story of our marriage. We have made our children here, and loved them in the peace-filled hours; yet this is the same place where we have inflicted wounds in reckless fury. It is where we say the things that we have been thinking for the longest time but have held in because to say them is to claw at the heart of someone we swore to love unto death. We spit those hate-filled words at each other sometimes, and this is often the place where we do it, even though it is our last refuge. I think that makes them hurt all the more, those words we hurl at one another, because we wield them in the place where we have made love and whispered their tender opposites and promised, in those myriad ways that married lovers have, never to leave. A poisonous word can be a yank on the bow's ribbon, unraveling everything with frightful ease.

Our bedroom, in the dark times of our marriage, became a battleground where Celeste and I laid out accusations like heartless indictments. We first uttered *divorce* in that room, not about some other couple, as if it were a disease that has struck, but about us, like it was a balm or a poison or both, lurking on the top shelf for years, and only now brought down and dusted off and held fearfully in our hands. For a time this was a nightly ritual in our bedroom—the anger, the hateful words, followed by resignation that there would never again be any way to climb over that wall that had risen up between us, a wall that had materialized seemingly all at once, but really over years. We would speak of divorce, sometimes in whispers, as if the children might hear us even though it is two in the morning. I think mostly we whispered because to say it louder would be to make it even more real, this poison cradled in our weary hands.

Nevertheless we sometimes stated it matter-of-factly, one or the other or both of us sick and ready to be done. At other times we hissed it, as if it were a weapon that could draw blood. During one of those nights I rose from the bed where we had been arguing and stormed over to my closet. "I'm done," I snarled.

"Fine," Celeste cried. "Get out." I threw open the closet door, grabbed a bag from the top shelf, and began stuffing clothes into it. I remember exhilaration, the adrenaline rush of knowing that in minutes I would be free. I would be in my car with my bag of clothes and the radio playing and the night air blowing against my skin, and there would be no more arguing or accusations.

Then it occurred to me that I had nowhere to go.

This wasn't a physical problem, of course. There are plenty of places to lay one's head. But I had nowhere to go, not really. I looked at the spectacle of myself, a grown man in a self-righteous huff, stuffing his clothes into a duffel bag that smelled of old gym socks. The truth is that there is nowhere else for me. Everything that matters is here, in this home. I looked so stupid to myself, in that brief moment of introspection, that I started laughing. "What's funny?" My wife asked, incredulous.

"I don't have anywhere to go." I giggled. I wish Celeste could have seen me in that moment as inconsequential, the way I saw myself. Then all the words and woundings up until that point might have carried less force. The cuts I'd made might have become shallower. Instead she was indignant. Maybe she thought I was laughing at her, or not taking this seriously. Perhaps she figured I was doing my usual thing, which is to make light of something rather than face the deadly dark center of it.

The funny thing is, I've never asked Celeste what she thought of my laughing that night. My skin crawls when I consider those nights spent fighting, all my deceptions, my manipulation. Recently I happened upon an email folder holding my correspondence with several men who did their best to pull me from this pit I dug for myself. I cringed at the lies I told even to them, as well as to myself. I deleted the whole lot of it. Perhaps a psychiatrist would say that it's not healthy, this shrinking from one's rotten past. On the other hand maybe it's best to lay that wretched old man down in the dirt and pray that Saint Paul was right, that we can be transformed by the renewing of our minds, that the old men and women we let ourselves become are now dead, thank God, and that we are miraculously becoming better people.

So I never asked Celeste what she thought of that night, what went through her mind as we fought, as she watched my aborted effort to pack up and leave for good. I only know that while I laughed for reasons I still don't understand, she didn't laugh at all. She wept like a scorned child, and miracle of miracles, she let her giggling idiot of a husband drop his musty bag and come to her in the bed. She let me wrap my arms around her and not let go.

She didn't laugh that night or for many weeks after, but her tears were different as I held her, my bag back in the closet where it belongs. They were softer, and for a few bleak hours we came to a truce as I tried to repair, just a little, the harm I had done. I don't remember anything I whispered to her that night, only the feel of her hair on my face, of her body bunched up tight in a ball, of her tears flowing onto her pillow as if all of her were going to spill out through her eyes. It was a long time after that night before she laughed again. Nothing is sweeter than the sound of Celeste's laughter.

Some months later I read the story about how Christ began winnowing his followers, revealing more and more of his outrageous doctrine so that even the ones who followed him for bread and protection would be forced to depart unless they embraced this radical God in their midst. "You will have to eat my flesh," he said to them, deliberately invoking something vile and unthinkable in that culture. And so most of his followers left, as he had known they would do. Preachers tend to render Christ's words with boldness and confidence from the pulpit, but when I read this story I imagine his voice is thin, and tired, and very sad. It must have felt suddenly lonely, to see all those backs turned to him. Then he looked around and found his twelve hapless disciples still lingering about, some probably embarrassed, others confused, at least one resentful. "Are you going to leave me too?" he asked them.

"Where will we go?" was the reply. I love the vulnerability and hope in that question, especially when so many of us who line the pews have made superheroes out of all these broken-down men and women of the Bible, forgetting that God does his work with the least of these, with the least of us. *Where will we go?* It's a way of saying, "We have nowhere left to turn," and also, "Even now you are the shining star." It's helplessness and hope all wrapped up together. This is what it felt like that night I told my wife: "I don't have anywhere to go."

While the shouting and arguing and threats of divorce seemed to be the dominant evidence of this home crumbling beneath us, it was the small things that sometimes stung the sharpest. The way we drifted apart in our sleep, for example, staking out two very separate territories on the edges of that bed where our daughter had departed from us. I said earlier that she had been a seam running down the middle of our marriage, and now that she had been plucked out we were coming undone. The quiet weeping of my wife in the dark, and the repugnant way I often pretended to be asleep so I wouldn't have to comfort her — or worse, simply lay there even though she knew I was awake. In that bedroom, in that bed, we learned to live apart while together.

I still don't understand why our marriage survived this. I don't know what to tell people who come to me from time to time, their own marriage in shambles, their bedroom a private war zone. I don't know what to tell them except the one word my friend wrote in a card after Caroline died: *Endure.*

This is not popular advice. Bookstores — especially Christian bookstores — are lined with volumes suggesting that marriage ought to be the deepest friendship, a source of great joy, a heavenly romance. If you are not happy right now, the subtext too often goes, then something is wrong and needs to be fixed. The standard, in other words — and despite all the God-talk in such books — is your happiness. Carrying this line of thinking to a natural end point, the new trend among some Christian speakers and writers is to wax poetic about the great sex married couples are supposed to have, as if one of God's deepest concerns is the quality of your orgasms.

The truth is that marriage is often a path of suffering. "From the moment you marry," said the Greek Orthodox priest Aimilianos of Simonopetra in a sermon on marriage, "you will have much pain, you will suffer, and your life will be a cross, but a cross blossoming with flowers. Your marriage will have its joys, its smiles, and its beautiful things. But during the days of sunshine, remember that all the lovely flowers conceal a cross, which can emerge into your sunshine at any moment.... It is an adulteration of marriage for us to think that it is a road to happiness, as if it were a denial of the cross."

Marriage is a daily dying to self, which is hard to reconcile with popular images of lifelong romance and mutual satisfaction. Endurance has been the way of man since the Fall—finding joy not in the absence of suffering, but in the midst of it. When Christ said, "Take up your cross and follow Me," he wasn't talking about a cute little gold cross that some people dangle from their chests as a signifier of their spirituality. Christ was talking about the sort of cross with weight and jagged splinters to which each of us nails his pride, his self-pity, his selfish wants, his dreams of how the world ought to treat him. Marriage is, for many of us, an essential part of our sanctification. In it we die, every day, for other people—for our spouses, for our children. Can joy be born in this? I can tell you that the answer, miraculously, is *Yes*. But not unless you endure.

Endurance wasn't, in our marriage, simply tolerating our growing apart. That's not really endurance, if you think about it — it's acquiescence. I had a friend who told me not long ago that he has reconciled himself to the reality that his relationship with his wife will always be hostile and unhappy. He said this as if it is some external reality over which he has no control. "You aren't accepting reality," I told him. "You're giving in." It's the opposite of endurance, even though it feels just as bruising.

Endurance was, for me and Celeste, performing the actions of love when we hadn't the slightest feelings of love for one another. Another modern lie, I think, is to equate love with a feeling. It's buried in statements like, *They fell out of love with each other* or, *Jane and I just aren't in love anymore.* In this we take our guidance from pop music when we ought to be seeking a deeper wisdom. God's love has never been just a feeling. It finds life through actions — wild, purposeful, outrageous actions — culminating in his living out his own definition of love, which is that a man will lay down his life for his beloved. We know love by its actions.

There was a night when Celeste cried uncontrollably at the foot of our bed, her spirit broken. I felt no love for her. I was trying to stay married nonetheless — for the children, I told myself in that hackneyed phrase — but I didn't have a shred of feeling for Celeste as I watched her weeping on the floor. I sat down and drew her into my arms all the same, not through any decency on my part, but from a sterile sense of obligation, the notion that this is what a husband is supposed to do. I drew her into my arms, and stroked her hair, and kissed her head. She turned into me, clinging tight.

I was overwhelmed, in that moment, with a sense of love and protectiveness for her. I don't know where it came from, and I would be lying if I claimed that it stayed with me in all the long hours and days and weeks of fighting to come, but the unbidden grip on my heart was real. What I learned that night is that enduring love is action, the laying down of one-self for another. Sometimes we are blessed with a deep sense of communion with the person we are loving, but other times not. If we wait around for a warm feeling in our tummies before we give ourselves to another, then we are never really giving ourselves at all. Love is action, and sacrifice, and self-lessness; how I feel is secondary to what I do. Love is, wrote C. S. Lewis, "a state not of the feelings but of the will, that state of the will which we have naturally about ourselves, and must learn to have about other people."

I can't be proud that I did, for once, what good men do. Celeste lived out love far better than I during those years. One time in the darkest part of night I woke to hear her whisper-ing; her hand rested lightly on my head. She was praying for me. She was praying that I would be healed of whatever poi-son was rotting me from the inside out, that I would be made whole, that I would be given peace.

I've never been betrayed the way I betrayed her. I've been wronged to a far lesser degree, however, and rarely has it crossed my mind, in the midst of my hurt and grievance, to pray for the person who wounded me. Yet this is what Celeste did for me that night, and probably on many other nights as I lay sleeping. It certainly wasn't because she felt magnanimous toward me. She did it sacrificially, living out a love that seeks not its own, but the good of another.

"But where sin abounded," wrote Paul, "grace abounded much more." I'd like to claim that our marriage survived because I pulled myself up by my moral and spiritual boot-straps and simply became a better man, the comforter and defender and one flesh of my wife, who endured my fury for years, along with my failures and sins, and yet still held on. But grace abounded, meaning that just as sometimes we are wounded without deserving it, we are rescued when we are undeserving. Grace is what saved our home, what saves any home and any soul — a holy grace that fills the breaks and crevices, making us what we were supposed to be from the beginning, which is the children of God. Celeste and I held on to one another, by the grace of God, and lived out love even after we'd stopped feeling it.

And gradually, the feeling came back, the way your breathing returns to normal and your head clears after a long illness. It came back the way sunlight breaks over the trees after a storm-filled night. It came back so strongly that I feel most at peace when I am with her, and not completely whole when we are apart. Grace abounded.

Grace was in the faces of our own children, floating crystal-clear in my mind at the moment when I most despaired, when I was ready to take my own life. Grace was in my wife who wouldn't give me over to self-destruction. Grace was even on the lips of my dying daughter, lips that named her brother, lips that reminded us, as we wept over her, that God says not to worry about tomorrow. Sometimes I wish I had a more secular answer, something that would make sense to every hurting person regardless of his religion or lack of it. But I don't. I have only my own experience, a recognition that many others have lived out as well, that in this ferocious love for our children is the love of a God who calls us his own.

Grace is in the small places, just as the despair was. It's in the way you wake in the dark of night and find that this person to whom you had become a stranger is clinging to you in her sleep, despite everything you've done. It's finding that you can't get out of bed for work until you have wrapped her in your arms, words not good enough, only this tight embrace coming close to explaining that she is life, that she is your one flesh. It's in the peace that settles over the bed when she is close to you, and your children are sprawled this way and that, and everyone is quiet, as if listening to something far away, a hymn perhaps—*streams of mercy, never ceasing, call for songs of loudest praise*—and you think:

Here is my every blessing.

Child! do not throw this book about!
Refrain from the unholy pleasure
Of cutting all the pictures out!
Preserve it as your chiefest treasure.
Child, have you never heard it said
That you are heir to all the ages?
Why, then, your hands were never made
To tear these beautiful thick pages!
Your little hands were made to take
The better things and leave the worse ones:
They also may be used to shake
The Massive Paws of Elder Persons.
And when your prayers complete the day,
Darling, your little tiny hands
Were also made, I think, to pray
For men that lose their fairylands.

Hilaire Belloc, "On the Gift of a Book to a Child"

6

Educating the Savages
the home classroom

Celeste and I don't like experiments. This is because our nerves are already frazzled from the merciless onslaught of injuries, spills, tears, cracks, and other forms of ruination that stem from living in a house with four mad young scientists. They experiment with how different household items sound when tossed from an upstairs banister. They experiment with objects — living, dead, and indeterminate — dredged from the bottom of our creek. They experiment with various methods of tumbling down the stairs, because walking with one's hand on the railing is, it seems, just not perilous enough. During cold and flu season one of them inevitably catches something and then passes it back and forth between his brothers, each of them refining the virus until it becomes some kind of superbug, at which point they pass their experimental creation along to us. They test everything from the fabric of their clothing to the lovingkindness of their thin-stretched parents.

You want to know why people who have raised children are more likely to vote for conservatives as they grow older? Because when you have worn yourself to the bone civilizing a

141

pack of beasts whom you were bound by law to let live with you, and along comes some smooth-talking, blow-dried elitist talking about *change*, you get an involuntary shudder. It's something akin to post-traumatic stress disorder, with the elfin voices from your past resurfacing: *Look, Mom, I cut my own hair. Hey Dad, I reset all the stations on your radio. Mom, Dad, why can't we go somewhere cool to eat for a change?* By the time your children are grown you've had just about enough change already, by golly, and the last thing you need is one more well-intentioned wiseguy shaking things up with his clever ideas. This is why I prefer politicians who look too tired to make any trouble.

Believing out of hope or desperation that the parenting skills we didn't learn in our own homes can be gleaned from *Little House on the Prairie*, Celeste and I are not just Old School, we are Rickety One-Room Old School. For all our talk about not rocking the boat, however, we have engaged in one of the most radical experiments a family can fit under one roof: homeschooling. I suppose it's not as radical as it sounds, given that Celeste was an outstanding teacher in public schools as well as private Montessori schools.

I'm sure Caroline is bound up in this somewhere. Maybe we have school at home not just because we think we can do a good job, but because we think they are safer when they are near us, or perhaps because we feel less empty when we are near them. Maybe we do it because we carry around an empty trunk that is called *Time You Did Not Have with Her*. Every hour stolen by death makes what remains more tenuous. I'm sure some selfishness exists in our decision to teach them at home, and so we try to counteract this by ensuring they have lots of interaction with other children, by involving them in a variety of outside-the-home activities, by making them take standardized tests to be sure we aren't permanently stunting their academic achievement.

Running underneath it all is the hope that more time with us is better than less, though in the dark night hours we've both wondered if even that is true. Maybe what we are is such a scarred-up, broken-down version of what we were supposed to be, after all, that our children would be better off with strangers. When you hear them laugh, or see them reading, or feel their arms around you, such a doubt seems small and distant, like storm clouds on the ocean's horizon. But sometimes those clouds draw close to shore, and you wonder if anything you do is right. You wonder if you are passing along all the bad things inside yourself, and if one day they will need intensive psychotherapy, and if when they are older they will avoid your calls the way you avoid many people in your own family. Maybe it's just a recurrence of that voice we learned to hear when we were children, whispering in our believing ears: *You aren't good enough.*

Whether we're teaching them right is a worry that preys on every parent, because in an important sense we are all homeschoolers. Even if your child goes somewhere else to learn his multiplication tables, he is learning from you the value of a conversation, or the importance of caring for the weak, or how to admit wrongdoing. Likewise, if he learns that his wants justify his actions, that behavior is less about being virtuous than avoiding punishment, and that watching television is an acceptable substitute for serving his fellow man, he is unfortunately learning all that at your feet as well.

The apple doesn't frequently roll far from the tree, and if that doesn't scare all of us parents into cleaning up our acts I don't know what will.

Raising children is a frightening responsibility, given how poorly so many adults turn out; but we parents of young children think of moral lessons as lurking somewhere off in their future. One day they'll come to us, puzzling over some difficult moral dilemma, and we'll deliver the perfect Bible verse to help make the right course of action clear. That's an easy enough fantasy to indulge when our immediate philosophizing about child rearing is concerned less with abstractions than with how to keep him from grabbing a handful of his own poop when one is changing his diaper. *Yes, concern for his fellow man will be important one day, but if only I could get him to stop putting his bowl of spaghetti on top of his head.* That's the kind of thing that goes through my mind when I think about training up my child, as the proverb advocates, in the way he should go. The way his mother and I want him to go is out of the house as soon as he turns eighteen, but no good college will take him if he keeps playing with poop and wearing spaghetti on his head—not unless he can kick fifty-yard field goals or hit twenty-foot jump shots. So we get consumed with the practical.

Celeste is the practical one in the family. One of her practical pieces of wisdom, for example, is that when it comes to potty training a child, the best approach is to simply take away his diaper. The theory is that once he has to choose between the potty and making a mess on himself, he'll opt for the path of Western civilization. Believe it or not, this actually works pretty well, so long as you are willing to spend a week or so following your little human sprinkler around with a roll of paper towels and some spray cleaner. We last did this with Isaac, which meant that for several evenings in a row when I arrived home from work I was greeted by a chubby little monkey in a sweatshirt and socks. "Hi, Dad!"

"Isaac!" I would kid him, my face taking on a look of shock. "Where are your pants?"

In reply his grin would get even bigger and he would squeal, as if it were the most delightful mystery in the world, "I don't know!" My sons have always found liberation in nudity. I hope that stops at some point.

The problem in Isaac's case is that his potty training got stretched out too long. We were in the midst of trying to sell our house, which meant frequent calls from the realtor informing us that we had to vacate the premises, which meant that contrary to our plan, Isaac alternated between nakedness and clothes. The result was that instead of teaching him to use the potty, we taught him to get used to the random discomfort of occasionally peeing on himself. He left puddles everywhere. It was like having a puppy—only a puppy can't climb atop a table and jump up and down like a lunatic midget until it crashes to its side, necessitating the boy's first x-ray before he can say "emergency room co-pay."

You would think a visit to the ER would teach the child a thing or two about being careful, but the hospital had Winnie-the-Pooh stickers aplenty, as well as a couple of pretty x-ray technicians who thought Isaac was adorable. So I don't think he learned a blessed thing from his injury, except that when you say "good-bye, ladies" to pretty x-ray technicians, they're likely to come chasing after you to give you one more hug and another Winnie-the-Pooh sticker for good measure. This does not bode well for when he is older.

We can set out to teach our children the simplest things—like not wetting themselves, and not breaking any more bones than absolutely must be broken to gain entrance into manhood—and make an utter mess of it. How are we going to get abstract principles right when even self-preservation is hard to teach?

Granted, potty training is not necessarily self-preservation for the child, but it certainly improves the parents' quality of life. Just consider the physics: When we began potty training Isaac he was in the third percentile for height, and the 96th percentile for weight. Do you remember the Oompa-Loompas from Willy Wonka's chocolate factory? If Oompa-Loompas had children, they would look like Isaac, only more orange. Isaac wasn't fat, but he was a thick chunk of barreling, screaming baby flesh. It takes a lot of food to sustain that energy level. Don't make me spell out the implication for Isaac's diapers.

Which raises another aspect of Isaac's training: During all this, Celeste was teaching him exclamations that are acceptable alternatives to what he had begun to pick up from his father. This came to the fore as I was changing a particularly lethal diaper. As the odor made itself known, I searched my vocabulary for an acceptable word, and in a poop-inflicted stupor I simply exclaimed, "Oh!"

Isaac took this as his cue to teach me a few phrases. "Oh boy! Oh bodder (bother)! Oh goodness! Oh mercy! Oh poo!"

"Amen to that," I muttered.

"Amen!"

Until Isaac, I'd never had a child so cute and such a terror all wrapped up in the same hyperactive bundle. Even now, two years later, he doesn't walk anywhere; he runs. He can't speak; he shouts. Food isn't eaten; it's horked down. He even tackles sleep like it's a bear that must be wrestled into submission. Everything is an adventure in Isaac's eyes. It's a good way to see the world.

The fact that I can't escape being a teacher is on my mind as I sit in a corner of a small music room, watching Eli with his violin instructor. She is a long-time public school music teacher, kind and competent and able to talk to little ones in a way that makes them feel special and heard, yet with a firmness in everything she does. She is incredibly patient, yet I get the sense from the wistful way she speaks of her grown daughter that things aren't very good between them. If someone like this has a strained relationship with her child, I feel tempted to despair over how my boys will one day view me. It seems so easy to get this wrong.

She listens while Eli tells her about Caleb's birthday cake, or shows her that the music notes look like balloons and golf clubs, or explains how his little brother thinks the chorus to "Old MacDonald" is "Eli-Eli-O." She always manages to steer him back to the task at hand without saying, "Shush it and pay attention," which is my too-frequent method. Sometimes when I watch her I am ashamed of my impatience. If this boy can be gently trained to sit still and learn the violin, why do I resort to bellowing when I want him to brush his teeth?

It's probably with Eli more than any of the others that I

have needed to learn how to apologize. My instinct for bellow-ing is the opposite of what he needs. When he was younger I used to position him before the toilet each night at bedtime. Eli sleeps hard, and I don't want him forgetting to go until he is playing with giant chocolate Lego blocks in Dreamland, where instead of toilets they have golden trees that sing Raffi songs when you pee on them.

One night after placing Eli in the bathroom, I left for a moment, only to return and find that he was bent over like an ostrich, his head almost completely in the toilet bowl. Hor-rified, I bellowed in that idiot-speak we parents have during our worst nobody-warned-me-about-this moments. "Hey, uh … boy! Unh-unh!! No, no, no, no, no!!! Get your, uh, get that, uh, get your *head* out of the *toilet*!!!"

Eli stood up straight as an arrow, his lip quivering. He grabbed his little blue blankie off the counter, and stood there looking at me with glistening eyes. I felt like I ought to be flushed down that toilet he was inspecting so closely. I kneeled beside him. "I'm sorry for yelling. Do you forgive me?"

"No," he whispered.

"I shouldn't have yelled. I just didn't want you to get any germs. Toilets are dirty. We shouldn't stick our heads in them. But I shouldn't have yelled. Did I scare you?"

"Yeah."

"I'm sorry. Do you forgive me?"

He thought about it for a second. "No."

I picked him up and kissed his soft cheek. "I won't yell again."

"Yeah, the next time I stick my head in da toilet, you won't yell at me."

"I won't yell, but you shouldn't stick your head in the toilet, okay?"

More thought. "Okay."

I never used to be an "I'm sorry" person, but there are some stretches in my parenting when I feel like it's all that should be coming out of my mouth. A friend who has raised several wonderful children told me that the secret is less in shaping them than shaping ourselves. Whenever he confronted something in one of his children that he knew didn't belong there—selfishness, say, or a spirit of anger—he soon discovered some corresponding darkness in himself that needed changing.

It's frightening and humbling, because much about me is bad right down to the core. Every time I pray that my children will follow a good path, I am praying for a miracle, because my own path is the one likely to exert the most pull. When I pray for them, I pray that I can set aside enough of my own wickedness to shepherd them for the scarce time they are mine. You needn't look to stories of fish and loaves for a miracle; look to the changed heart of a man.

I used to think that I could raise my boys to have honor, strength, and grace without attending to those qualities in myself. That's impossible. If we want our children to do justice, love mercy, and walk humbly with their God, then we have to do the same. This is why I decided some time back to oppose something the company I work for was doing that I believe is wrong. It wasn't a violation of law, but of their own self-declared principles. I knew challenging it would cost me goodwill, if not more. I was sorely tempted to turn my gaze elsewhere.

Then I began to think about what I would want my sons to do. It's not like they'll know their dad turned a blind eye to wrongdoing. But I'll know. That's the catch. If I stay quiet when I believe wrong is being done, then I have been a coward. A man can't be a coward, or hate-filled, or faithless, and not have his children see it. And they love us so much that they try to become us, even if what we are is reprehensible.

Most of the time I am a coward. But because I love them, that day I tried to be something better. It didn't do one lick of good to walk into the CEO's office and tell him I believed the company was doing something it shouldn't, but at least that day I wasn't a coward. It's just one day stacked up against scores of weakling days, but it's a start. Maybe we can be something more than weak, and broken, and dark-hearted. Maybe we can. *Where I am weak, He is strong.*

Some preachers imply that faith is all that matters. By faith you are saved; have faith in Jesus and you will be washed clean; keep the faith. But the Bible also says that faith without works is dead. When you consider that works are intimately bound up in faith, and further, that as a parent your path is the easiest for your children to follow, then a hope and a prayer isn't enough. Waiting and endlessly preparing and ruminating on holiness isn't enough; we have to do the slow, painful separation from the path of the world.

I wonder, if we kept in the front of our minds that "holy" means "separate," would that change anything? Holy doesn't mean being good; it means walking the separate path, our eyes on the narrow shoulders of that God-man who walked before us. Anybody can be good, especially when we let good be defined by the safe, church-going masses; but to be holy—well, that is another matter, isn't it? The separate path is dangerous. No good parent wants to lead his children into danger, but our choice is either to walk the holy path or let the world usher them down its well-trodden fairway. We can't send them off to do what we failed to do; we can't just hand them a Bible and a sack lunch and wish them well. We have to walk the path ourselves.

I suspect I may fail at this holiness thing. Anyone can see by this point that my track record is terrible. So I pray that it's the trying that matters, the desperate striving, and throwing ourselves at the feet of grace. There is redemption in the striving, I think. I hope so, for my sake, for their sake, for yours.

Right now the sun is shining, the older two are reading, and their younger brothers are pretending to read. The learning possibilities seem limitless, and so today we are confident homeschoolers. We are official homeschoolers too, having registered our school (the Woodlief Homestead School) as required with state authorities, attended home-school conferences, stocked up on materials, and even invented some of our own. We teach the boys in a room upstairs that we call, not so imaginatively, "the classroom." Right now it's mostly Caleb and Eli who do schoolwork there, though Isaac spells and draws and generally behaves like a student until something shiny distracts him. Baby Isaiah understands that his job is to grab hold of people's legs and snatch pencils from desks and caterwaul whenever he gets ignored. His mother informs me that he deserves an A-plus for his efforts, and that she may very well lock him inside a closet until he is five.

I remind her that we're preparing the boys for the real world this way, because really, when can any of us remember the last time he got to read a book or compose a letter uninterrupted? If it's not your baby pestering you it's your boss, and probably more than a few of us can discern precious little difference between the two. Usually when I say something like this, Celeste offers to trade places with me and brave in my place that dreadful "real world" I frequently bemoan. Adult conversations, lunches without squawking babies, a steady paycheck to affirm one's worth in the world — she says she believes she can handle the "stress" of my daily work life. I reply in a magnanimous tone that I love her too much to inflict that on her. She rolls her eyes, and I quickly change the subject. I know I have it good.

It's easy for me to be enthusiastic about homeschooling right now because in these early years most of the education is my wife's domain. She is masterful at teaching small children how to read, and most important, how to learn, cultivating in them an essential combination of discipline, confidence, and joy. I'm on the hook soon enough. It begins with languages, which we determined should be mine by virtue of the fact that I am a writer, and therefore presumably gifted with words. A great many writers, of course, disprove this assumption, not to mention the fact that about the only foreign language I know is a single sentence in Spanish: *Mi llamo Antonio y llevo los pantalones grandes*: "My name is Tony, and I wear the big pants." It seemed like a useful pickup line at the time.

I also know enough French to get me arrested in several parts of Europe, North Africa, and a smattering of Asian countries. My lack of language skills, however, is not relevant, apparently, to my assignment as language instructor by virtue of the reality that my wife will hurt me if I try to defer all my teaching responsibility to their teenage years. So I have become the designated languages instructor at the Woodlief Homestead School.

The beauty of home education in the twenty-first century, however, is that you can do a decent job without years of professional training—and judging from what passes for a curriculum in many university schools of education, you may do a better job. *Gracias a Dios por la Piedra de Rosetta.* Another benefit of homeschooling is that you get to learn, along with your children, all the things you didn't pick up during high school because you were preoccupied with chasing girls. Right now I'm learning to read music in Eli's violin lessons, and by this coming spring there will be more to my *Español* than an ineffective (as it turns out) come-on.

As the boys get older I will pick up still more of the teaching load, becoming the resident dean of literature, politics, history, theology, logic, writing, and debate. I'm also the in-house karate, wrestling, and boxing instructor. Since I can barely bounce a basketball or swing a bat, we'll be outsourcing the rest of their physical education. I'm enthusiastic about teaching them at home, but I'm not an idiot.

Enthusiasm aside, I should stress that our home is not a well-oiled educational machine. It is, in fact, a whining, groaning, often shrieking machine. Most of these sounds come from our children. Caleb has mastered what I call the Art of the Ignoramus, which is to pretend that he just doesn't understand the instructions, or that he didn't quite hear you, or that he forgot what you asked him to do each of the last five times you've spoken to him.

Caleb's occasional intransigence leads to scenes like this: First, I come home and intuit that his mother is irritated. I am able to do this because, as her life mate, I am attuned to her every emotion. The smoke coming from her ears is also a clue. Next, she explains to me that we are not going to homeschool anymore, and further, that we are giving Caleb up for adoption. Because it's much easier to be the rational parent when one hasn't spent an entire day with the children, I suggest that perhaps I should talk with the boy first. This is followed by a growl, which always makes me marvel at Caleb's willpower, because I would never deliberately get on this woman's bad side.

In the classroom I find Caleb hunched over his desk, a scowl on his face. He sees me, and launches into a discourse, likely rehearsed, about the unreasonableness of his mother. "I told her that I don't understand, Dad, but she won't listen." He recounts his strenuous efforts and his mother's ferociousness, along with an analysis of precisely what's impossible about his schoolwork, rendered in detail that's remarkable for someone who claims not to understand what he's supposed to do.

It's probably helpful at this point to note that Caleb comes by his stubbornness honestly, and not from his father.

What follows is something very much like police hostage negotiation, or perhaps Middle East peace talks, with me in the hapless role of Jimmy Carter, offering appeasement at every turn, along with ridiculously complicated accords, all of which are geared less toward a long-term solution than a short-term stability that will allow me to declare peace and read my newspaper.

A year ago I came home to find them both near tears. Caleb was seven at the time. "He's been sitting there all afternoon," my wife explained, "complaining about his math work. If he would just focus he could be done in twenty minutes." I adopted my best U.N. peace commissioner face and entered the classroom.

Caleb was waiting with the most pitiable face he could conjure, his excuses at the ready: his brothers were too loud; the work was too hard; his eraser didn't work right. I told him there would be no dinner until his work was completed. I told him I was getting this from the Bible (implication: *Don't blame me*), where Saint Paul admonished: "If anyone will not work, neither shall he eat." It seemed like the right kind of threat: stern, biblical, but unlikely to be triggered. I offered to Caleb that I would wait for him to finish, so he wouldn't have to eat alone. What's an extra hour of waiting, I reasoned, if in return I, the wise, firm father, can have some quality time with my chastened, peace-filled child? I was sure, you see, that even this boy wouldn't be so stubborn as to miss out on dinner. I sat like a self-satisfied Pilgrim and read my newspaper.

I was wrong about the ability of hunger to focus this boy's mind. As bedtime approached I realized that Caleb believed he was being persecuted. Apparently a part of him enjoys martyrdom. (Celeste, having read a draft of this chapter, wants me to note that this particular trait does *not* come from her side of the family.) It was one of those innumerable parenting moments when you aren't sure what to do. If Caleb really thinks I'm being unreasonable and that the work is too hard, isn't it overly harsh to punish him? On the other hand, if I relent, doesn't it just reinforce his wrong impression about the difficulty of the work, and teach him to give up, and to deceive himself about what he can or cannot do? Maybe I shouldn't have made that "no dinner" threat. If only I had an instruction manual.

With a sick feeling in my gut, I told my son that he would be going to bed hungry. My bluff was called. Every movie I've ever seen about cowboys or poker indicates that you should never get caught bluffing. I suspect the same goes for parenting.

After his initial wail of grief and horror, I explained to Caleb that he wouldn't die from missing a meal, though he was quite certain that he would. Through his sniffles he peered up at me to ask if I was going to eat. I sighed. I could smell dinner waiting in the kitchen. "No," I told him. I squatted down to peer into his watery brown eyes. "The fact that you didn't get your job done today is proof that I haven't done my job very well."

I think this satisfied Caleb's sense of justice, or perhaps commiseration. He leaned into me and burst into tears. I helped him get ready for bed, and tucked him in, and prayed with him. Later I prayed—a little louder to drown out my growling stomach—that I wasn't being a terrible father. It's one of my fears, that I will lose my job and be unemployable and my children will go hungry. And here I was denying my son food. Do good parents do that?

I suppose we can err on either side of consequence. The world is a causal entity, after all, and every action—and inaction—bears consequences. Our job as parents is to expose our children to this harsh, consequential world without letting them be killed or scarred. As I write this I think of Eli's forehead, which has a circular scar from a straw. Don't ask me how he did it, I still can't quite understand it myself. The thing is, we want them to learn how gravity works without breaking their necks, and how fire works without setting themselves—or the house—ablaze; but how are we supposed to teach them consequences safely when even a straw can be dangerous? Yet if we protect them from too many consequences, we send them out into a world that will abuse them. They will be permanently dependent on us, which is a cruel thing to inflict on one's child.

But what if we are too harsh? Should every mistake carry a punishment, every slip a rebuke? This is a hard, embittered world we live in, yes, but it is a grace-filled world as well. How do we show them the way to live on this earth except by making our homes a place where just consequences are intertwined with the beautiful injustice of grace? Neither Celeste nor I knows exactly how to do this. It's the home we want, but it's nothing like the homes we come from.

I know some parents who are quite adept at balancing consequences and grace. My friend Steve was raised by parents who were firm and loving, who expected him to live with the consequences he earned for himself, but who tempered this justice with mercy. He knows how to discipline and how to give grace in equal measure because this is how he was parented. His oldest son recounted the conversation with a college admissions official about his transcript, which included both home-school and private-school grades. "He wanted to know how I got that one B, when the rest were A's. I told him my dad gave it to me."

"And you earned it," was Steve's reply. He had no problem denying his son a perfect transcript. He'd always stood ready to add extra work to his son's already considerable list of responsibilities on their farm, as a means of teaching him a lesson about sloth or disrespect or work ethic. Surrounded by an excuse-laden society, Steve doesn't tolerate excuses. Yet his son knows Steve loves him more than life.

I've watched Steve for years. He doesn't realize it, but he's the one, probably more than anyone else, that I try to emulate as a father. I wish I could point to some enormous decision he made, some profound life event he manufactured to bring up his children well. Instead, discouragingly, it turns out that Steve is a master of small moments. He is a good parent because he was raised by good parents. His instincts are good. He fathers deliberately and well, and you can see it in the countenances of his children.

My instincts, on the other hand, are shot through with selfishness and sloth. I get angry when my children disobey, not because they are sowing the seeds for a hard life down the road, but because they have impugned my sense of personal grandeur. I get irritated when they make messes because it inconveniences me. I'd rather they play outside than try to help me with a home repair because that way I can get it done faster. My instincts are all wrong.

So always doubt plagues me: *Am I doing this right?* When Caroline lay sick in bed, no longer able to speak, I put my head on the pillow beside her one night and whispered to her that I wished I had been a better father. I wished I had been more patient, had played with her more, had taken her on every errand. I suppose I was apologizing as well that she was sick, that she was dying and I could do nothing to heal her. It's entirely irrational, and yet many parents of dead children feel it, a deep gnawing sense that we have failed them. They look at us in those last moments of life as if they are clinging to a fraying thread, as if we can pull them back to safety if only we would try harder, but we can do nothing but stare back into their fading eyes and watch them leave us.

It's a silly thing, to worry over one missed meal. I suppose it's not that meal I'm fretting about, or the last time I barked at one of them, or the time I put them to bed in a rush because I wanted to watch a movie. It's all of it together, this parenting that feels for all the world like drawing with the wrong hand, or swimming out past the dock where the water is colder and darker, where you begin to wonder if you have the strength to make it back to shore. *Am I doing this right?*

The morning after I sent him to bed hungry, Caleb rose early and got his work—which the day before had been a confusing, intricate, impossible assignment—finished lickety-split. Then he had a nice warm breakfast. I've never broken a fast that filled me so much as knowing food was going into my son's empty tummy. Maybe that's how God feels about all of us. Maybe communion is as much about filling him as it is filling us.

I am filled this way as well when I come home to the peaceful air of little minds set on their paths, reading or doing math or practicing their spelling. They look up and smile, or perhaps Isaac shouts, "I doin' schoolwork!" and shows me a picture. In such a moment, when I see Eli figuring out logic problems well beyond his age, or happen upon Caleb reading *The Swiss Family Robinson*, and he looks up to tell me that we should build a Woodlief family tree house, the doubt is gone, and I know we are doing the right thing.

I recall JCPenney marketing a T-shirt a few years back with "Homeskooled" scrawled across the chest. JCPenney is headquartered in Plano, Texas, which doesn't exactly qualify anyone to be uppity. When I see my children in our classroom, working dutifully at their lessons, I am reassured that they will emerge better educated, and certainly with better manners, than most JCPenney executives. As a matter of fact, if I had to choose between JCPenney stock and Woodlief boy stock, I know where I'd put my money. In a way, I guess that's what we're doing.

Something I'm learning as we forge ahead with this homeschooling experiment is that children are sponges. This is true in more ways than we like; my own little sponges make a regular habit of spreading chewing gum, pine tar, and semi-congealed apple juice, among other pernicious substances, on their fingers and in their hair and on the bottoms of their shoes. We know this by the unidentified patches of stickiness that crop up throughout the house, in particular on their mother's antique sofa. But children are also sponges in an intellectual sense — how else could an infant learn both a language and how to work the remote control by age two? I, on the other hand, barely know the one language and have yet to understand most of the buttons on the remote. I guess my sponge is drying up.

The thing about a sponge is that it will soak up whatever liquid comes into contact with it. At a very practical level this means that, as Celeste used to say during her years as a kinder-garten teacher, "Your children will tell your business." If they aren't telling your business to strangers in the grocery store, they are totally selling you out to your spouse. Like the time when Celeste was walking with the boys across the parking lot at Walmart only to have Caleb protectively grab her arm and point at a passing minivan. "Be careful, Mom," he cautioned. "It's a woman driver."

To make it even better, my mother-in-law was with them.

Or consider the time when, upon passing the detergent aisle at the grocery store, Caleb announced to his mother, "This is the Mommy aisle."

"Why is it the Mommy aisle?" inquired my wife, no doubt recalling the woman-driver comment.

"I guess because God made you that way," replied my son.

I still insist that he didn't get that idea from me, but I don't think I make a very persuasive case. I suppose a little male chauvinism goes with the territory in this house with five males, the older ones of whom are constantly asking when we can drive off in my truck or go play in the woods and have some "man time," which is to say, "no girls allowed," which is really to declare, when you break it down, "no moms allowed." I'd feel bad for Celeste if a rest from the whole lot of us wasn't exactly what she wants.

It doesn't seem fair that the kids remember something I mumble under my breath while driving, but can't internalize my deliberate instruction. Sometimes I have a brief and rare flash of wisdom that I feel I should impart to the boys. I think of these as my Clark Griswold moments, after Chevy Chase's loveable character in one of my favorite movies, *Christmas*

Vacation. Once I tried to explain poverty and thankfulness to four-year-old Caleb and two-year-old Eli. "See kids," I intoned in my best Clark Griswold voice, "some children don't have many toys or clothes or even food, but we have been blessed with all kinds of good things. That's why it's important to be thankful, and to take care of our belongings, and to give some of what we have to people who need it."

"What?"

Sigh. "Caleb, didn't you hear anything I just said?"

"Be thankful."

"Yes. And what else?"

"For children."

"No, I said—"

"I thankful for my blankey, and airplanes, and my ship..."

"No, no, no, Eli. Daddy said be thankful for the children."

"No, I didn't. I said some children don't have—"

"I thankful for the children, and my blankey, and airplanes, and my ship..."

"No, Eli, it's *my* ship. He thinks it's his ship, Daddy."

"Listen, boys. Listen. You both need to get in the habit of being quiet when Mommy or Daddy is talking, and listening to our words. No more interrupting. Listen to what we say."

"What?"

I'm hard-pressed to think of a more demoralizing word. You work up a good head of steam as a parent, and lay out the Almighty Truth for them plain as day, clear as a bell, maybe for the first time in your entire parenthood, and that is— inevitably—the time they don't hear a word you've said.

What? Caleb can wield that question like a punch in the gut. He's a daydreamer, so he uses it often. Thankfully, I am not always the victim. Once we were in the grocery store, being tended by a cashier whose shirt was emblazoned with "WORD" in bold letters, under which was stenciled a revolutionary fight-the-power diatribe of the sort that inspires skateboarders and the judges who hand out Nobel Prizes for literature. Caleb was still too young to read, but he knew what letters are for. Ever the sociable type, he asked, "What's your shirt say?"

I think the cashier saw this as his opportunity to hit us with some knowledge. He pulled the shirt away from his chest so he could look at it more clearly, and began to read his manifesto to us. It was a weird and awkward moment. I was trying to think of a diplomatic way to cut the lecture short when Caleb set him straight. "No, no, no. I don't want to hear all that." He thrust his stubby finger toward the top of the young man's shirt. "What's that big word say?"

"Well, uh, 'word.'"

"Oh. That's nice."

And that was the end of the speech. The cashier finished ringing us up, mumbled, "Have a nice day," and we went about our business. It was nice to see Caleb nip someone else in the bud for a change. Maybe there's hope yet. And I like to think that in some way his quest for bottom-line clarity in that instance was something he inadvertently soaked up from me. Because God knows he doesn't seem to hear anything I say to him directly.

I guess in all this homeschooling and training and hand-wringing over whether we're getting it right is a desire not just for our children to be well-educated, but to have good hearts. We are working out how best to train them—in our classroom and in every other room as well—not only to help their intellects flourish, but because part of building a home, we are learning, is training our hearts and the hearts of our children to seek God where he will be found. Wendell Berry argues that schools ought not to focus just on imparting skills, but on cultivating humanity. "For human beings the spiritual and the practical are, and should be, inseparable." Training up the heart is more important than teaching the mind, and this is what we are wrestling out each day, on the battlegrounds of our own hearts as well as theirs. "I would rather have a boy of mine stand high in his studies than high in athletics," wrote Teddy Roosevelt to his son, "but I could a great deal rather have him show true manliness of character than show either intellectual or physical prowess."

This classroom is where we are preparing them to understand the world—and to be forces in it. Some days it is like an insane asylum—what with the drooling and doodling and Celeste the warden, who is sometimes an inmate herself. Other days it is the most peaceful of places, each boy quietly reading or drawing or doing a science experiment, and we are filled up, Celeste and I, with the sense that this is what we were made to do, to teach these children, and to be healed by them, even as we train them to be healers in a broken world.

There's always something I can do
To pass the time away;
The dark comes quick in winter-time—
A short and stormy day
And when I give my mind to it,
It's just as father says,
I almost do a man's work now,
And help him many ways.

Sarah Orne Jewett, excerpted
from "A Country Boy in Winter"

7

Open Range
outdoors

Somehow Celeste and I decided that it would be healthier for the boys if we lived in the country. Neither of us can give you a clear train of logical thought to justify this conclusion. We can't exactly articulate how leaving our comfortable suburban home to dwell on twenty acres in the boonies is a good decision. When we talk about it with people we toss out words like "real work" and "wildlife" and "adventure," but we usually do this without considering the fact that for every nature-besotted family choosing to relocate away from civilization, there is a country family which has decided: *We're sick of the dirt road and no cable TV and mud everywhere and the spiders and the snakes and not being able to make a Taco Bell run when we get the late-night munchies.* For every suburban slicker betting that country living is the life for him, there's someone with muddy boots who doesn't want to play "Green Acres" anymore.

It's the mowing that gets to you first. Before you have time to kill yourself in a freak chainsaw accident, or drown while mucking out your lagoon, or get tangled up in your own barbed wire, it's the innocent-looking grass that will lay you

167

low. More specifically it's the heat and dust and 87 varieties of Kansas pollen that all conspire to kill you when summer comes. M. Night Shyamalan made a film called *The Happening*, in which plants set about poisoning humans. Most people figured it was too far-fetched to make a good movie. These people are welcome to come mow my front yard in the midst of wheat harvesting season.

A good part of our property is creek and trees, and right now we keep only the house and barn side of that creek cleared. This is because there are skunks and bobcats and the occasional coyote out here, and these are all creatures you want to see coming from a long way off. At first I tried to mow this area with an old riding mower given to us by Celeste's grandfather. This thing moves about as fast as Eli eats his broccoli, and with even less enthusiasm. It also does that gagging thing that Isaac stages for dramatic effect when we make him eat squash.

When he saw me putting around on this asthmatic mower, the only neighbor within eyesight of our property felt so sorry for me that he fired up his tractor and brushogged alongside me as I mowed. He left a wide swatch of destruction in his wake, while my mower sputtered and complained and suggested we move back to the suburbs. My neighbor rode up high in his cowboy hat and boots, and I in my baseball cap and old running shoes hunched over my little mower like a kid on one of those pretend motorcycles you see going in circles at the state fair. My neighbor with his calloused hands, and me with a single callous on my pencil finger. It dawned on me that I don't compare so well to the average country man. I realized it was going to take some work to blend in out here.

Take brushhogging, for example. It took me a while to figure out what it is, but I picked up pretty quickly on the fact that real men are in favor of it. They are also in favor of tractors, and so I borrowed one until we can afford our own. It sits higher, eliminating that toddler-at-the-fair feeling. It has a big mowing deck. It actually seems to enjoy working. If I let this tractor sit too long I can hear it growling and questioning my manhood when I pass by.

Our recalcitrant riding mower, meanwhile, mostly just sits in the corner of our barn and sulks. Eventually we are going to transform the old geezer into a racing vehicle — I have this on Caleb's authority. He explains that it will be a relatively simple procedure, having read in a book about how to do this. I hope the boy's mechanical competence grows to match his ambitions, because sometimes I have trouble getting a light bulb screwed in properly.

This is a source of enduring embarrassment for Celeste and me, that I am better at cooking and ironing, and she more mechanically inclined. If there is a lamp that needs rewiring, Celeste is your gal. Come to me if you want lasagna or perhaps an amusing anecdote. I can even touch up your sleeve creases while I tell it. Unfortunately, however, Celeste feels unwomanly when her chicken comes out of the oven with less moisture than the Sahara, while I feel unmanly when I install a sink only to have every single pipe joint commence to leaking as soon as the first little boy washes his hands.

We both have watched enough movies where men are nurturers and women are nuclear physicists with black belts to know that it's hip to break gender roles. Nor do we hold one another to them. I consider Celeste's knack for home repair not just admirable, but downright sexy. Her disinclination to cook is a bonus, because it means more pizza nights than I would have enjoyed were I married to Rachael Ray. And I bet Rachael Ray doesn't know how to mud and tape. There is nothing hotter than a woman who knows how to put up wallboard. When you live with four boys, you need someone who can repair holes in walls.

For her part, Celeste seems to like that I wanted the six-hour BBC version of *Pride and Prejudice* for a Christmas present. She loves it when I take over at breakfast and whip up omelets for everyone. She understands that I have no interest in learning exactly how our furnace works. And she doesn't consider me less manly for being unable to overhaul a Chevy transmission.

At least that's what she says.

Ever have a thought like that flit through your mind immediately after someone gives you a compliment? Self-doubt is a haze that distorts any light trying to pour through. No matter how much I insist to Celeste that seeing her in a tool belt makes me want to kiss her, that aprons and oven mitts are unattractive, that so long as she gives me mac and cheese once a week I will be a deliriously happy man, she can't forgive herself for not knowing how to make spaghetti sauce from scratch. This is not because she believes spaghetti sauce is the key to real womanhood, but because she grew up thinking she wasn't good enough. Not good enough to warrant uncon-ditional affection. Not good enough for her parents to let her join a program for gifted children when she was invited, or to let her go on an all-expense paid trip to London with her own grandparents, or to cast out the man who was preying on her.

It's a subtle poison that seeped into her skin, as it does many children. It's acidic, etching into your mind: *these good things are not yours to have.* If anyone tells you what a fine job you've done, think instead on your failings. When someone gets angry at you, instinctively assume he is right to do so. If someone offers you love, remember that he doesn't really know you. Maybe that's what keeps so many of us running from God—his awful claim to know us, as he peers out from beneath his blood-stained brow, whispering with thirst-swollen tongue that he loves us even now, even as he hangs on his man-fashioned cross. We run away shaking our heads and bitterly chuckling, thinking nobody in his right mind can look into the black hearts we secretly carry in our chests and still love us that way, that we can be loveable only so long as nobody really knows us.

It's not just her past to blame. My compliments would mean more if I hadn't lied to her so very often that I lost track of what was true. I told her she was beautiful when I was cheating on her. I told her she was the only one when she wasn't even first on the list. In narcissistic moments I am taken with the notion that I am the hero of a romantic novel in which there is some mountain I can climb to make her believe she is lovely, some river I can forge so she will know she is just right for me, some beast I can kill to prove she is worth everything. But the mountain is my own ego, the river my self-seeking, the beast within me. These are the things that prey on her now, the things within my power to stop. Somewhere in our marriage—maybe from the very beginning—I became the poison.

And so when I labor outdoors I have two purposes. One is

based, as a good friend explained long ago, on the simple fact that hard work wards off the demons. Work yourself without relent until there's no daylight left, and then get yourself into the home where your woman waits, and you'll find it hard to get in trouble. It was when King David became lazy, after all, that he got into that bloody business with Bathsheba.

The second purpose is related to the first: I work because it makes her feel worthwhile. Yes, it's good to keep the grass sheared and the fence mended and the dead trees cleared. The truth is, though, that I could live amidst incredible disrepair and tell myself it's rustic. Thoreau got along fine without a chain saw. But when Celeste sees that I have tamed a small part of the world for her, knowing as she does that I'd rather be reading Wendell Berry than working like him, I think she believes, just a little, that she is worth it after all.

I don't enjoy all the outdoor work, but I'm trying to keep this from our children. That's because I harbor a dream of one day looking up from my computer to see all of them outside, cheerfully mowing, cutting, harvesting, and otherwise doing all this work for me. In this dream they are also skilled cooks, and so after baling hay they come inside and make me some penne pasta with tomato sauce. Perhaps my own outlook on work has been irrevocably sullied, but there's no reason not to try and cultivate in my sons love for an honest day's labor.

Most children seem to have an innate capacity to enjoy creative labor, at least until our own grumbling and slacking teaches them otherwise. So I figure the task is not to implant some alien feature—love for labor—in my boys, but instead to work on not being such a sourpuss about it myself.

It was Caleb who first taught me that a child can see work much differently than an adult. I needed to install pull-down steps and flooring in our attic. It's more accurate to say that Celeste *wanted* this done, which meant that what I *needed* was for her not to hit me with my little-used hammer if I put it off another weekend. So I grumbled and cursed those steps into place, and then set about trucking floorboards up to the attic. That's when Caleb, who was four at the time, appeared at my side. He had on a yellow hardhat made of plastic, and a tool belt containing an assortment of tools and toys. He informed me that he was ready to work.

Too many times I've barked at my children to let me be so I can get some work done. I remember telling Caroline to leave me alone so I could work. I remember her crestfallen look, and the way her hair hung in her face as she slowly walked away, head down, arms at her sides. What I can't remember is the work itself, the tasks that were so important that I needed my daughter gone.

You'd think I would have learned my lesson, and never again griped at one of my children to let me be. But I am thickheaded and selfish, and so my instinct when Caleb offered his help was to send him to pester his mother. For once, however, I had the good sense to recognize that fatherhood was offering me something rare and easily missed. I nailed down a section of flooring, and then helped him up the steps. I positioned him beside a low wall, and told him to have at it. He took out his little hammer and commenced to whacking the floorboard.

As I installed additional sections I kept an eye on him to be sure he didn't wander too far and fall between the joists.

It was hot that day, and soon we were covered in sweat. I quietly cursed my splinters, and the heat, and the scratchiness of fiberglass insulation that found its way inside my clothes. Caleb had put down his hammer in favor of a tiny paintbrush, which he was dipping into his tray of watercolor paints and applying, one pale stroke at a time, to a long stretch of wall. He hummed while he painted.

I still remember that job as one of the most miserable home improvement projects I've ever undertaken. I was itchy for a week, and my back ached for twice as long. Celeste added to the punishment by giving me load after load of stuff to store up there. She smiled a lot, and talked about what a gift it was, and so I felt like a hero nonetheless, albeit an itchy, achy, grumpy one. Months later, Caleb was snuggled up in my lap. "Dad," he said, "do you remember when we worked in the attic?" Yes, I told him. My neck instantly recalled the itchiness. He squeezed me tight. "That was fun. We should do that again sometime."

Have you ever been filled with pride and shame in the same breath? It struck me that the real task in front of me is not this home repair or that yard project; it's bringing my children alongside me so they can learn how to do work well and cheerfully. I resolved then to work harder at engaging my children in work. They have to learn how to peel carrots and work a socket wrench somewhere, after all. What's more, if Caleb could come away from that stifling attic with a fond memory, then maybe these boys can grow up enjoying all kinds of labor. Maybe I have more to learn from them, in fact, than they will learn from me.

Isaac, for example, has taught me once again to love

mowing, the way I did when I was a kid. That's probably too strong; his bliss, when he is wearing froggy boots and pushing his plastic pretend lawnmower, counteracts my grouchiness, yielding something like satisfaction. It also helps that my physician equipped me with a high-powered nasal spray to combat the toxins with which Mother Nature is trying to murder me. Even with the drugs, mowing would at best be tolerable, but to Isaac it holds some kind of magical appeal. His zeal is more catching than the worst of allergies.

When we had just the little riding mower, Isaac would demand to ride in my lap. We would pass back and forth across the lawn, his legs growing numb from sitting funny, and my leg shrieking with pain every time he shifted positions and ground his butt-bone into my thigh. When I would run out of gas and be forced to set him down, he would wobble and rub his legs and begin to cry because they had fallen asleep. But still he persisted in riding with me as often as I would let him. Sometimes he would fall asleep that way, forcing me to balance him on my lap like a sack of potatoes.

Even when we lived in the suburbs, it took a few hours to mow and trim everything. The Kansas sun burns hot, but just like Caleb in that attic, Isaac stuck with me when I mowed. He didn't come along just for the riding part. When I retrieved the push mower to get around trees and alongside the house, Isaac would fetch his plastic version and follow behind me, faithfully covering every square foot I mowed. When I got out the weed trimmer he would slip on his goggles and lay hold of a plastic hockey stick to use as a pretend trimmer. At the end of the afternoon, as I gulped down ice water and waited for a heart attack, Isaac would stand beside me with a plastic cup of his own, his face red as a beet, his blond hair bunched up on his head in a sweaty tangle.

And he would smile. A big cheese-eating grin, like there is nothing better in a little boy's world than to spend five hours with his dad, cutting grass under a blazing sun. Even if you can't bring yourself to love work, you can appreciate how magical it is to have a child love you like that—so mightily that he thinks hard labor is the greatest blessing and gets more and more excited as the grass grows so he can go out and do it again. I can tell when he has missed me or when he wants my attention, because he will quietly get out his plastic mower and begin pushing it around our yard. I hope he will think of me when one day his own children are following him around his yard, and that they will look at him as he looks at me in these waning days when he still thinks I am a superhero. One day maybe he will realize that he is the superhero, and that even as he wants to be like me, I wish I could be more like him.

Isaac was in awe from the moment we backed that tractor down the trailer ramp. At first I wouldn't let him ride on it because it was new to me, and big, and I was a little afraid to be behind the wheel myself. Our land isn't flat like it was in suburbia, and there are places where I worried about tipping over. I told Isaac he would have to watch, not ride.

It would have gone better had I filled his Christmas stocking with turnips. Forbidding this child a tractor ride was like telling Dale Earnhardt, Jr. he has to drive an ice-cream truck. It was like taking away Martha Stewart's fabric swatches, or

Ernest Hemingway's typewriter and liquor bottle at the same time. Eventually I relented, reasoning that I was experienced enough now to be safe, especially on the flat patch of land where I first hauled Isaac up onto the rig.

The tractor manual has some tips for avoiding rollovers, which I studied carefully. Every community has stories about farmers planted into the dirt by their own tractors. I know to be cautious on hillsides. What the tractor manual doesn't explain, however, is that the roll bar jutting up behind your head—required by law for your safety—can actually be the death of you. Thus Isaac and I go bouncing across our yard on the tractor, oblivious to the fact that we are passing beneath lower and lower tree branches.

Until that roll bar catches on a thick limb of hedgewood. Your instinct, when you observe the front of your tractor rising into the air like the nose of a jet during liftoff, is to hit the brake. So your foot leaps to the left. That's where the brake is in your car. The brake on this tractor is somewhere else. Instead of finding the brake, my foot catches the tip of the accelerator. The tractor's front wheels are now a foot off the ground. The tractor shudders. I realize we are either going to flip over backwards or that branch is going to come down on our heads. The dark thought passes through my mind that I am about to get my son killed.

I'd like to report that I uttered a quick prayer and did something brave and wise, but instead I blurted a curse word, grabbed Isaac tight enough that he almost pooped, and hit the clutch in hopes that something good would happen. Perhaps an angel is assigned to watch over idiot, not-so-gentlemanly farmers like me. Maybe Isaac had been extra-diligent at his bedtime prayers. Or perhaps it really is true that God won't break us down beyond all repair. That's what would have happened, had I killed Isaac with that tractor. I heard a cracking, tearing noise above our heads, and the bottom of the branch sheared off. The tractor's front wheels came down with a thud. It took a little while before I could let go of my son.

I still feel sick to my stomach when I think about it. Celeste asked me once, as Caroline's death approached, if I thought this would be the hardest thing God ever asked of us. I told her I didn't know, but like her I imagined that we were somehow being inoculated against the world's tragedies. A parent can only endure so much, after all. Surely God wouldn't let another of our children die, would he?

You think this after you have buried one of your children, and then you meet a parent who has lost more than one child, or read about some poor father whose entire family is killed in a car accident, and you realize that whatever heartache you've suffered isn't like a dues payment at all. The world is always looking to take more from you. There is no inoculation against heartbreak.

When Caleb was two he was at the top of the steps leading to an apartment over our garage. I was up there fixing the door, and he was, as usual, sticking by my side. I heard him slip, and as I turned he went tumbling beneath the guardrail and over the side. He had a dazed look on his face as he disappeared from my view. I cried out his name, and looked over the railing to where he lay facedown in the dirt, ten feet below. I don't know what I yelled as I ran down those steps two and three at a time, but I think it was a combination of cursing and calling out to God and saying, "No, no, no." I remember what was going through my mind, however, because it was directed at God: *How could you?* I demanded, and, *Not another one.*

I don't know what I would have done had he lain dead in that dirt, any more than I could have told you, when Caroline was still here to do a happy dance on pancake mornings, what I would do if she left us. We never find out what we will do in those horror-filled moments until they are upon us.

When I reached Caleb he was trying to sit up, dirt in his mouth and eyes, blood coming from his nose. I swept him up and took him to the house where Celeste and I cleaned his face, checked his arms and legs and fingers for broken places, and examined his pupils. He began to chatter and smile before we could decide whether to take him to the hospital. I didn't have to find out that day what we would do without Caleb; but I was reminded exemptions don't exist. If you love anything, you must live with the reality that one day you may lose it.

I think the fear of losing my kids is always somewhere on my mind, which is why I can only pretend to read as Celeste and I sit in lawn chairs on a sunny Sunday afternoon. Across the grass, Eli is swinging baby Isaiah John. "Not too high!" I shout. "Make sure he holds on!" Isaiah John is squealing with delight. Isaac runs toward them, with a look in his eyes like he intends to see exactly how high this baby can swing. I warn him off. He moans and does his slump-shouldered, limp-armed walk toward another swing, where he plops down and glares at me like I am the Yard Grinch.

Eli is swinging Isaiah John too high again (says I; Celeste

disagrees). "Too high, Eli! Too high!" Now Isaac has rustled up a stick and is trotting over to his brothers to do God knows what with it. "Drop the stick!" I sound like a police officer now. "Put. The stick. Down. Step away from the stick. Do not. Touch. The stick. Again." More slump-shouldered groaning intended to communicate that I am The Meanest Dad Ever. I pretend to read some more, except that now I am glancing up every five seconds. This is not, I don't think, the Sabbath the Lord had in mind. He just had the one kid to look after, mind you, when he first started this day of rest thing. Perhaps he had higher hopes for it.

Or maybe I should just relax. This is Celeste's advice. I blame this cavalier attitude on her lack of imagination. I can think up five ways, easy, that Isaiah John could get killed on that swing. And don't even get me started on the calamities that might befall someone if we let Isaac run around with sticks in his hands.

I know my worry has shifted into overdrive, that it does this sometimes. I spackle what is supposed to be a relaxed smile across my face, and tell Isaac to fetch us some cookies. "Don't start eating them until you get back out here!" I shout after him. Otherwise he might forget and just sit in the pantry with them.

Now he has returned, and we are all eating cookies, the children clustered around Celeste and me in our lawn chairs. The dog ambles over, and I go to grab the cookies to keep her nose out of them. My jerking movement topples my drink into the cookie tray, which with this new liquid weight topples off the chair's arm and directly into my lap. I am covered with lemonade and soggy cookies. The silence is strained. Celeste and the children are watching me, their mouths twitching, perhaps trying to decide if Dad is finally going to have that big mental breakdown they've all been waiting for. Then they laugh. They are covering their little cookie-stained teeth with their hands and giggling. Even the dog looks to be laughing.

I suppose it's funny. I allow for the possibility that I, who have been fussing at everyone for the past half hour to be careful, might just be worth laughing at.

I'm getting better at laughing, I swear. Take the time I let the older boys wash my pickup truck, only to come outside and find them missing. My truck was there, covered in rapidly drying suds, but my truck-washing labor had disappeared. Then I heard giggling, which is when I noticed that the water hose was stretched up into the truck bed. As I got closer, I could see the shimmer of water in sunlight, which is when I noticed streams of water dribbling from the tailgate seams. Water splashed as Eli popped his head up, then Isaac, then Caleb, like three mop-headed otters. They had turned my truck bed into a swimming pool. Even a grouch like me can laugh at that.

This is not a farm pickup. It is my snazzy Toyota Tundra, purchased used but shiny, in part to make up for the emasculating effect of our minivan. Because it is shiny, and because it is mine, I don't always appreciate what my children do to it when I am not looking. Like when I find muddy footprints all over the windshield, only nobody can quite remember walking on Dad's windshield. Are you sure, Dad, that it wasn't some *other* kids from some *other* house? Or the time I noticed Isaac's toolbox on top of the cab, only to discover when I climbed up to investigate that he had carved dozens and dozens of scratches into the paint with his screwdriver.

"Isaac!" I shouted. He came running to me. "What did you do to my truck!?!"

He saw the ugly anger on my face and began to cry. "I don't know!"

I lifted him up to the truck bed where I stood, and then held him over the cab so he could see his damage. I wasn't very gentle. "I am very angry," I growled. "You've ruined the paint!"

"I'm sorry!" he wailed.

"What were you thinking?" I didn't wait for an answer, I just went on like this for a minute, barking and yelling, exclaiming about the cost of paint and how ashamed I was that he had used his tools to do something so naughty. He just stood there in my truck bed and cried. When I was done with my tantrum, he held out his arms. "I sorry, Dad. Do you forgive me?" He said it with little hitches between the words, the way children do when they are trying to talk and cry at the same time. I felt like an ogre as I knelt down for him to rush into my arms. "Yes," I said begrudgingly. "I forgive you."

"I was trying to scrape the stickies off," he explained. He meant the spots of pine tar. Spots just like the ones I had gotten him and his brothers to help me with months before, using plastic pot scrubbers to scrape the hood and front bumper. He'd found some more pine tar on the top of the cab, and he wanted to be helpful. He didn't see any difference between a pot scrubber and a screwdriver. He thought he had done something that would make me happy.

Now there was no question about it: I am an ogre. I scooped Isaac up into my arms and asked him to forgive me. He put his arms around my neck and squeezed, his fat warm cheek pressed into my jaw. He forgave me because he doesn't know any different, because he hasn't yet learned—thank God—that nothing in the world can make us forgive, and everything in the world mitigates against it, most venomously our ideas of justice, and our inflated sense of self-importance. But he hasn't learned any of that. Even if I teach him nothing else I pray I won't teach him unforgiveness, though I've been guilty of it more times than I can count.

Parents carry two buckets: one full of the things we hope to teach them, and one full of the things we hope they never learn from us. In that second bucket I carry unforgiveness and anger and a selfish heart that too often loves things more than people. So I hugged Isaac close and kissed him once for every hundred of my sins, or maybe every thousand, only before I could finish he was giggling and pushing my face away because my goatee is scratchy. This is how a parent's penance is, I suppose, never enough to satisfy us, yet more than they asked for.

Grace is like a flood, and I know floods because it has been raining hard for two days and our house is surrounded by water. The creek spilled over its bed sometime this morning, and now the water is rushing past the corner of our house, spilling across our driveway, and reconnecting with itself on the other side. A piece of play equipment floats by. It's from a wooden play structure that we bought for our church after Caroline died, using money people donated for some kind of memorial. We figured a play set was a good memorial to Caroline. The church didn't want it after they bought a new building across town, and so it's been sitting in pieces behind our barn. Now it's floating away.

We tell the children to stay put, and Celeste and I go wading out into the water. Soon we are up to our waists, leaning forward against the cold, hard current, salvaging what we can. The pieces of wood are heavy. We drag them one at a time inside a fence enclosing our barnyard. We hope the water doesn't knock the fence down. More pieces float downriver. We grab a hobbyhorse, and then wrestle the trampoline to higher ground. We are covered in muddy water, and the rain is coming down harder now.

I walk over to where Celeste has just pushed a beam toward the soggy grass. She is breathing hard and wiping the rain from her brow. I take her face in both my hands, and I kiss her. She puts her arms around me, thinking it no more strange than I that we should be standing in the pouring rain, knee-deep in flood water, making out. This is our marriage, I think, as we stand in the thieving water that wants to drag us downriver along with the things it has already stolen from us. Feet planted on treacherous ground, holding on to each other, praying that the water won't rise much higher. We are all of us praying, I suppose, that God won't let the water rise too high.

We are inside now, looking out one window and then another, watching the water swirl around our house, wondering if it will breach the flood wall on the back side, if it will creep up our driveway until it is pouring into our basement from front and back. I have moved my truck to the other side of the water, in case we have to run away. We don't know what we'll do if the water keeps rising. None of us knows, does he? But for now it is holding steady, which is maybe all any of us can claim as well, that we are holding steady, neither rising nor falling. We are holding steady inside, the boys pretending the house is a sailing ship, Celeste and I tensely praying, and outside the rain keeps falling heavy enough to keep us worried, but not hard enough to breach our fragile walls.

Our walls hold. The damage is minor, nothing like what those poor people suffered in New Orleans, watching helpless as the merciless water carried off everything, sometimes even their loved ones. Ours was a tempest in our little Kansas teapot, which is what most suffering is, when you think about how this world of wicked men martyrs the helpless every day. Maybe all my worrying will one day make me more grateful as I consider how bad things could be. That seems a churlish way of going about it though, a backhanded way of thanking God for grace poured out in the form of four boys and a beautiful loving woman and this life that is more than I ever thought I would have. I'm trying not to worry, because worry is a sin. Instead I'm simply trying to ... breathe.

Like now, sitting on our driveway in the late afternoon, where the children wield relatively harmless but scary-looking pumpkin-carving implements. Isaac is jabbing at his pumpkin and I am breathing in and out, and trying to think less about punctured eyeballs and pumpkin-seed choking incidents and more about the fact that each of us is carving a Halloween pumpkin, which is one of those Family Moments that I ought to have the good sense to enjoy without a knot in my stomach.

Isaiah John sits nearby, having given up in frustration on his effort to get someone to let him hold a pumpkin. He is swatting a chubby hand at the midges, which are drawn to the little piles of pumpkin guts that litter our driveway. "No!" he says to the midges. "No, no!" The midges aren't obeying.

Isaac (with his mother's help) carves a standard jack-o'-lantern, with triangle eyes and nose and a single tooth. It has an enormous stem jutting upward like a lock of hair, as if it's stuck its finger in a light socket. This is why Isaac picked it out at the little country grocery that has better prices than the popular pumpkin farm we visited earlier this week. Caleb uses a stencil from the store to carve an elaborate spider diagram in his pumpkin. It's not any fun, to Caleb, unless it is complicated. Eli carves a menacing yet slightly mournful face into his pumpkin. He and his pumpkin look wistfully at one another.

I am the designated pumpkin mortician, and so after hollowing out each gourd I follow with my knife the design Celeste has etched onto the biggest pumpkin — the Family Pumpkin, we call it — to produce a goofy face. Later we wash and dry and toast the seeds, and set the Jack-o-lanterns on our back deck with candles in their bellies, facing the house so we can see them. The four of them grin up at us, and we grin back.

I like it when we do this, when we stand inside the warm light of our home and peer out at the gathering dark. I don't know why it makes me feel safe and brave and slightly sad all at once, but I want to live this way with them forever, and sometimes I wonder if heaven will be like this, if we will stare out at the black universe from God's house of gold and light, and know that the darkness is banished from our lives forever and ever, amen.

I hate ingratitude more in a man
than lying, vainness, babbling, drunkenness,
or any taint of vice whose strong corruption
inhabits our frail blood.

William Shakespeare, *Twelfth Night*

8

Listen

the doorstep of heaven

Eli makes bookmarks and gives them to me. He makes long skinny ones and flimsy square ones. Sometimes he cuts out a raggedy circle, or an awkward heart. He colors his creation as best he can, or draws a picture of us playing together. On some he writes things that he would never say out loud, like, "Dad, I love you so much." Sometimes he fashions his gift out of a scrap sheet, and other times he uses scalloped scissors to craft his bookmark from a thick piece of art paper. He leaves them for me on my nightstand, or my desk, or sometimes he overcomes his shyness and gives one to me directly, saying simply, "I made this for you." When Eli does this I wrap him up in my arms and squeeze him for an extra-long time. This is how you have to hug Eli, because he can be like hardened ground that the rain takes longer to soften.

Last year Eli gave me a flashlight for Christmas. So did Caleb. They know I already have one under my bed, another in my nightstand drawer, and a little one on top of my dresser. I guess they believe a man can never have too many flashlights. I suppose they're right. When your piece of earth turns its back to the sun and darkness settles on you like black snow, you want more than anything a little scrap of light to show you the way.

When Isaac gives me a gift it is inevitably chewing gum. I'll find a foil-wrapped stick on my computer keyboard or nuzzled up beside a book I've been reading, and I'll know Isaac has been thinking about me. Sometimes he sidles up next to me with a pack of gum in his hand, sporting an expansive air, looking for all the world like a tycoon tipping the doorman as he peels a stick from his gum wallet and drops it in my lap. Chewing gum is Isaac's favorite. He would take gum over ice cream or even cake. We limit his gum intake—the current rule is that he can have it only on Sundays—because he never spits it out without an explicit instruction to do so, and with four children it's hard to remember that your four-year-old has been chewing the same piece of gum for ten hours.

I suppose our strictness about gum makes it all the more precious to Isaac. This is why he can't think of a better gift to give to someone he loves. My instinct would be to hoard something that precious, the way I'm reluctant, for example, to offer guests my favorite—and expensive—brand of chocolate-chip ice cream when I've been lucky enough to find it on sale. Isaac's instinct, however, is to share the things that are precious to him.

I've been thinking about these gifts from my children. Homemade bookmarks, cheap flashlights, and a few sticks of gum are hardly worth including in the nation's gross domestic product. Neither, I suppose, are the few quarts of grape juice or wine, along with the handful of bread or crackers, that you will consume in a lifetime of taking communion. Somehow in our supersized culture we came to believe that if God were real, he would manifest himself like a rock star. Occasionally a preacher or a singer comes along and gives us that rock-star God experience, but mostly the things of God are manifested in the murmur of a priest or preacher, the croaking of a congregation's song, the sometimes blissful and other times dreadful silence of our prayers.

We have forgotten the God of small things, which is mostly what he has been with us because we are ourselves small, fragile things. We wait impatiently, sometimes hopelessly, for the burning-bush God, or the booming thunderclap God, forgetting that even a righteous man like Job cowered before the whirlwind of God's voice, that holy Moses could bear only a glimpse of God's backside. We assume that we would hold up well against a visitation by the whirlwind God, and in our narcissistic longing we forget the God of the still, small voice, the suffering-servant God, the God who said of children that his kingdom consists of such as these. "Part of the inner world of everyone," writes Frederick Buechner, "is this sense of emptiness, unease, incompleteness, and I believe that this in itself is a word from God, that this is the sound that God's voice makes in a world that has explained him away. In such a world, I suspect that maybe God speaks to us most clearly through his silence, his absence, so that we know him best through our missing him."

So what are some flimsy paper bookmarks, two hard plastic flashlights, a stick of gum still warm from being kept too long in a little boy's pocket? By the standards of this world they are nothing, and yet they are everything to the man with eyes to see. "I was blind," wrote the wretched slave trader John Newton, "but now I see." Long before him, Saint Paul wrote,

"For since the creation of the world His invisible attributes are clearly seen. . . ." How can God's invisible attributes be clearly seen? Perhaps they are invisible because we look in the wrong place, on the wrong terms, with wrong expectations. Grace is in the small places, if it is anywhere. "Paradise has simply clothed itself," goes a hymn by the Syrian Christian Saint Ephrem, "in terms that are akin to you." Later he writes:

> *The breath that wafts*
> *from some blessed corner of Paradise*
> *gives sweetness*
> *to the bitterness of this region,*
> *it tempers the curse*
> *on this earth of ours.*

Perhaps to speak of earth's bitterness is too negative for some; but who has not tasted it in his suffering? If you have not suffered then you have not lived, for to persist on this earth is to endure the brokenness of things, perhaps chiefly the brokenness of ourselves. But still a sweetness blows from heaven, grace in the small things.

Eli makes bookmarks because he sees the books piled about my desk and nightstand, on my dresser and even—to Celeste's frequent consternation—atop the rows of books lining our otherwise neatly stacked bookshelves. He gives me bookmarks because he knows I am afraid of losing my place. I've spent at least half my life trying to find my place, and a good portion of the other half losing it. I'm sitting here with Eli's bookmarks spilling out of my hands, a flashlight on my desk, a bent piece of gum beside it. I am run through with the miracle of these children. Flesh of my flesh, dreamers of my dreams, little fumbling heroes. They are my bookmarks, each of them. They show me where my place is in the world. I was blind for the longest time, but now I see.

And if the light starts to go dim, I have a flashlight, and more than that, the sound of their voices, which is imprinted on my mind like a melody. I can hear them now even though they have all gone to town with their mother, leaving Daddy alone in his small office built into the corner of our barn. They know I am writing about them, and they have been reminding me of stories I ought to include. They don't quite understand why I am writing all this down, other than the obvious fact that surely everyone in the world will want to hear about them. In this they have inherited the narcissism of their father.

On the same Christmas day that Caleb and Eli each gave me a flashlight, Celeste gave me a cross made of two nails welded together and polished. I saw it at an arts-and-crafts fair and dropped a subtle hint, something like, "Hey, why don't you buy me that for Christmas?" Celeste has always been attuned to my nuances.

I like this cross because it has some heft to it. I used to wear a small cross made of light stone, but there were plenty of times I forgot it was there. I can feel this one thump against my chest when I walk, and poke my skin when I twist the wrong way. Crosses are only what we make of them, I suppose, if that. Some people like small crosses tucked beneath a shirt, others like a bold crucifix dangling outside their vestments. As for me, I like this simple cross of nails against my skin. At times it is the slightest bit painful, and its weight keeps it never far from my mind. I've done my blackest deeds when I put the cross far from mind. I need this weight, just like I need my bookmarks and flashlights and love offerings of sticky chewing gum.

Celeste and I are preoccupied with our own mortality. I suppose when you have a child in the grave, your thoughts run more frequently to death, and what lies beyond. Also, I am a hypochondriac. This is a recent epiphany for me, and when it dawned on me how frequently I turn headaches into life-threatening meningitis, or muscle spasms into incurable cancer, I made a point of sharing it with Celeste. I was proud of the introspection, after all, that led to my discovery. I laid it all out for her, connecting the dots between my ailments and my — as I understand now — frequent mutterings about this heart palpitation being a sign of heart disease, or that mole seeming to have moved in recent weeks. "I think," I said earnestly, "I might have hypochondria."

When you refer to yourself as having hypochondria like it is itself a deadly illness, you have proof that you are a hypochondriac.

Celeste laughed at my revelation. "Do ya think?" I hadn't realized it was that obvious. I appreciate that she's kept this knowledge about me to herself all this time, but now I wonder what other of my flaws are glaringly apparent to her.

This hypochondria is relatively new, I am fairly certain, because not so long ago I was ready to die. Now I fear death, not because of what I expect to find on the other side, but because I don't want to leave my boys before they are grown. I'm probably overestimating what I bring to their lives. I fear death all the same, because they love me so much that sometimes their fast-beating hearts seem ready to burst with it. I don't want them to grow up without me.

I feel like a bull in a china shop, surrounded by this love of theirs, with my every careless gesture and irritable scowl threatening to break something irreplaceable. Sometimes when I am thinking the worst of myself, I imagine that maybe they would be better off without me. I figure the ache of my absence couldn't be as bad as the pain of my presence, considering my grouchiness, my occasional bad-tempered barks, my frequent desire to read rather than play Tickle Monster. I don't think I am often a very good father. Yet they love me all the same, and they would miss me terribly; and like everything else that might cause them grave harm, I fear this too: that I will be taken from them while they still need me.

So I examine my moles obsessively, and pay extra attention to my cholesterol, and check my pulse after a sack of fries to see if that final, fatal, inevitable coronary blockage is going to kick in. I view every doctor's appointment like running a deadly gauntlet and turn each minor ailment into the first salvo of something far more gruesome. The behavior is self-reinforcing because once you have been this vigilant (Celeste would say "paranoid") for so long, you start to think that the first malady about which you don't obsess will — ironically, because we are an irony-besotted culture — be the one that does you in. Worrying becomes, in a twisted sense, an inoculation against disaster.

I understand that I need therapy. Perhaps a whole team of therapists, working around the clock.

Celeste's preoccupation with death, meanwhile, is at once

more positive and more gloomy. It's more positive insofar as she has no fear of it. She has always been fatalistic, and on top of that, at least vaguely Calvinistic, and so she believes her time will come when the good Lord is ready to take her home. The gloomy part of her is that she is more than ready for that time to be today. Or tomorrow. Maybe next week. In your time by all means, Lord, but let's not tarry, okay?

I suppose she is tired, because she has had more than her share of hardship. She has suffered the three great betrayals this world hurls at women—the loss of her parents' protection, the death of her child, and the treachery of her husband. We are better now than we were, but I don't have any illusions about anything I ever say or do making the scar I've inflicted disappear. She is tired, and I know I am part of the reason.

Celeste is less worried about leaving behind the children than I for the simple reason that she has an even lower opinion of her mothering than I do of my fathering. "You can always find someone to tutor them, and to cook, and to clean," she says in her Eeyore voice. She talks this way when she wants to pretend to joke about how much easier life will be when she is gone, even though we both know she isn't joking. "Then eventually you'll find a better wife."

When she does this I roll my eyes at the implicit melodrama, or I get mad and scold her not to talk that way, or I announce that there is no way ever that I am getting married again. This last is a bad direction for the conversation, because she hears it as a critique of her in particular, even though I mean it as a statement about marriage in general, and more to the point, about me. I am not a pleasant person to live with, of this I am pretty sure. So why spend all that time and energy trying to fit myself together to some other woman whom I'm only likely to make miserable? The altruistic thing would be to take myself off the market.

Not that Celeste is going to die before me, because as I write this I am battling a lingering cough that I am pretty sure is lung cancer. True, everyone in the house has had a cough too, and it is cold and flu season; but I think my cough sounds different. If this book is published posthumously you'll know my worries were finally justified. That's the side benefit of hypochondria, by the way; eventually you end up being right.

Celeste begrudgingly agrees that she will likely live to be ninety, because she figures that's another way God will find to punish her. We both still suffer from the temptation to think of God as sitting up in heaven shrouded in a cloud of disapproval that rumbles in response to our every failing. We tend to imagine that if things have gone well for too long, he's going to correct course by zapping us with a tragedy. It's the legacy of too much bad theology, coupled with a naturally gloomy outlook in both of us. I hope we don't pass this kind of thinking on to our children. Maybe if we both dropped dead they would have a shot at being raised by people who aren't neurotic pessimists.

Then again, I'm meeting more and more parents who have the same suspicion that someone else could do it better. Maybe that's because we all see the wretchedness inside ourselves, but very little of what resides in other people. We fall into the error of thinking that what we see of others—which is almost always the best of them—is what they mostly are. And we conclude that our best, which of course is what we try to show other people, is really just a contrivance, and not part of the real us.

Maybe it's closer to the truth to admit that the times when we force ourselves to be loving and patient and selfless — even though it can be a struggle — are really part of who we are just as much as the us that snaps at our children. And maybe we'll all of us have a better view of our fitness to raise children if we remember three things: that everybody messes up, that our children love us in spite of it, and that God gave us particular parents these exact children. These little ones are from beginning to end blessed mirrors reflecting what we are and what we strive to be. I don't believe God is accidental about the children he gives to us.

So while I don't feel worthy or fit to raise Caleb, Eli, Isaac, and Isaiah, I know that for some inexplicable reason, God believes I am. And he believes you're worthy and fit to raise your children too. Are you going to argue with God? Trust me when I tell you that never ends well.

Mom," Eli asks Celeste at dinner one evening, "who do you love the best?"

"I love all of you the same."

"But which one is best?" chimes in Isaac.

Celeste laughs. "You are my best Isaac, and Eli is my best Eli, and Caleb is — "

"No," says Eli, the logician in the family. "You can't love us all the same. Who do you love best?"

Perhaps a better husband would intervene at this point in an effort to help his wife extract herself from a jam, but I'm curious to see how she's going to wiggle her way out of this one. I certainly don't know how to explain to them how it's possible to love each of them fiercely, yet for different things. Caleb the earnest inventor, Eli the gentle dreamer, Isaac the rampaging Viking, Isaiah the roly-poly clown—who knew it would be possible to love each of them so fully, and with a broken heart, no less? I don't know what Celeste is about to say, but I hope she can explain it to me too.

"My heart," she tells them, "is a house filled with rooms. And each of you has a room all to himself."

Each boy smiles, perhaps considering what his room in Mom's heart must look like. Maybe they imagine rooms full of toys, a comfy bed, all their stuffed animals. What a little boy can't know, until he has children of his own, is that his room cradles every giggle, every sigh, every squawk, all those skinned knees and scuffed shoes, each dream carelessly or cautiously shared, all the hopes we have for them, every prayer we've whispered over them in their sleep. The rooms of our hearts are full with everything that is them, and when we think back to the days before we had them, we realize how much smaller our hearts were back then.

I am standing in our backyard as the last golden sunlight pours through the trees. They don't have leaves yet, but spring is coming. Some days you can feel life returning before you have any real proof. You can smell the warm air beginning to find its way through the creaking hedgewood, feel the topsoil softening as it comes awake, almost hear the sparrows flying home. Life is returning to this cold, barren place, and with it you can feel something inside you being restored as well.

It's only for a season. You know that in the months to

follow you will, God willing, see the once-green leaves flare out yet again and fall dead to the ground, watch the sparrows depart once more, feel the cold air rush back in to embrace you as it tries to do even now. You know that one day beyond that the cold will return just for you—no matter the season—that your heart will strain to beat once more, and perhaps try to steal another beat after that, and then it will stop. The people who are still on earth to love you will weep over your cooling body, and then they will tuck you into the earth. We look to spring with joy because it reminds us that life springs up from the sleeping earth. We ease our loved ones into the ground, just as we will one day be placed beside them, in the hope that death is no more the end than a frigid winter wind is the end of all our springtimes.

It is only a season. This is only a season. One day I will breathe my last, and I will be tired no more, no longer filled with fear, finally certain of something. I will slip away from the sound of my heart's dying rhythm, and this will be finished. I believe in a God who loves even the likes of me, and so I believe I will wake once more after my body betrays me, to the sound of singing. I am sure the songs of angels must be beautiful, but it will be the warbling of a little girl that my ear searches out. It has been so long since I have heard her voice. It has been so long, but I needn't wait forever. Spring is coming, a spring with unfading colors, enduring warmth, life that doesn't mourn its own passing.

The temporary spring of this waiting earth is coming as well, and the day has been warm enough to open some windows. I can hear my children laughing inside. They are setting the table for dinner. I listen to the clang of silverware being set down too hard on the table, the squawk of Isaiah John as someone stops him from collecting all the just-placed silverware into a tangled pile, which is what he likes to do. I hear Isaac's belly laugh, and Caleb's voice as he attempts in vain to direct his brothers. I see a flash of golden hair as Eli passes in front of a window. I hear above all of it the steady voice of their mother. She loves me, and I don't know why. I think it's time just to accept it, to accept the love of these children and this God I don't understand. We struggle to accept the curses of this broken world, and sometimes we struggle to accept the blessings as well. I'm going to do a better job of accepting them both.

Once I prayed that God would do me the kindness of letting me sit on his doorstep just so I could hear my children in heaven. It occurs to me that this is what it might sound like, that in a way he has given me what I asked. Only the door is open for me, and inside they are waiting. It is more than I deserve. It is more than any man deserves. This is exactly what God does, because he loves us as we love them. Where there is love, what we deserve has nothing to do with it. The door is open, the table is set, and I hear someone calling my name. I am going inside this simple house now, this home that has become somewhere more holy than I thought was possible. Someone is calling my name, and I am coming home.

Years ago, my friend Michael Bankston gave up his career teaching art for a corporate job, in order to provide for his growing family. He had not touched his brushes or pencils for nine years when, after the death of our daughter Caroline, he bought three pieces of art paper and sat down with her photo. His hope was to practice on the first two pieces and create something suitable on the third. What you see here is a photo of the portrait he created on his first try, which he gave to us on the anniversary of Caroline's death. It hangs in our home today. Though for many years Michael sacrificed his art for his family, he is now a full-time photographer, doing once again what he loves. Celeste and I are thankful to him beyond words for this picture, as well as for the cover art to the book you are holding.

Credits

The author and publisher gratefully acknowledge the following contributors for the use of their work in this book:

Bradshaw, Melissa and Adrienne Munich eds. *Selected Poems of Amy Lowell*. Copyright © 2002 by Rutgers, the State University. Reprinted by permission of Rutgers University Press.

Jeanine Hathaway, "IN THE BEGINNING". Original poem, used with permission.

Albert Garcia, "August Morning," *Skunk Talk* (Bear Starr Press, 2005). Originally published in "Poetry East," No. 44. Used with permission.

Ruth Moritz, "Caravaggio Light." Original poem, used with permission.

Charles Lamb, "Parental Recollections," *The Works of Charles and Mary Lamb*, ed. E. V. Lucas, III (London: Methuen, 1903). Public domain.

A. F. Harrold, "Room Poem, #1a." Used with permission.

Excerpt by Hilaire Belloc from *Verses* (© Hilaire Belloc, 1916) is reproduced by permission of PFD (www.pfd.co.uk) on behalf of The Estate of Hilaire Belloc.

Sarah Orne Jewett, "A Country Boy in Winter," *Harper's Young People*, January 24, 1882. Public domain.

William Shakespeare, *Twelfth Night*, 1623.

Share Your Thoughts

With the Author: Your comments will be forwarded to the author when you send them to *zauthor@zondervan.com*.

With Zondervan: Submit your review of this book by writing to *zreview@zondervan.com*.

Free Online Resources at
www.zondervan.com

Zondervan AuthorTracker: Be notified whenever your favorite authors publish new books, go on tour, or post an update about what's happening in their lives at www.zondervan.com/authortracker.

Daily Bible Verses and Devotions: Enrich your life with daily Bible verses or devotions that help you start every morning focused on God. Visit www.zondervan.com/newsletters.

Free Email Publications: Sign up for newsletters on Christian living, academic resources, church ministry, fiction, children's resources, and more. Visit www.zondervan.com/newsletters.

Zondervan Bible Search: Find and compare Bible passages in a variety of translations at www.zondervanbiblesearch.com.

Other Benefits: Register yourself to receive online benefits like coupons and special offers, or to participate in research.

ZONDERVAN®

ZONDERVAN.com/
AUTHORTRACKER
follow your favorite authors